MW00438422

THE STORY OF ISLAMIC IMPERIALISM IN INDIA

THE STORY OF
ISLAMIC IMPERIALISM
IN INDIA

SITA RAM GOEL

VOICE OF INDIA
New Delhi

ISBN 81-85990-23-9

© SITA RAM GOEL

First Published in 1982
Second Revised Edition 1994
First Reprint 2001

Published by Voice of India, 2/18, Ansari Road, New Delhi – 110 002 and
printed at Rajkamal Electric Press, New Delhi – 110 033.

CONTENTS

CHAPTER I

IN THE NAME OF NATIONAL INTEGRATION

Comrade Radek, whom Stalin liquidated in the late 'thirties, was a Communist intellectual endowed with acid humour. He coined many jokes at the cost of the Communist Party and the Soviet State. One of these jokes which did the rounds in Moscow was as follows:

One day Comrade Radek stood stark naked in the Red Square in broad daylight. A courageous citizen approached and asked him, "Aren't you afraid of the police, Comrade Commissar?"

Radek stared at him, and shot back, "Police? Where is the police?"

The citizen pointed towards a number of policemen positioned on all sides of the Square, and said, "There is a policeman. There is another. And yet another...Why, the whole place is crawling with policemen."

Radek replied, "You can see them. I can't. I am a party member. I am not supposed to see them. For party members there is no police anywhere in the Soviet Union."

The ruling class of secularists and socialists in India today is in a similar situation of ideological blindness. It is not supposed to see the violent waves of Islamic imperialism surging all around it. That would be a sacrilege and a serious slur on its reputation as progressive, liberal, and large-hearted.

It is in the living memory of this ruling class that Islamic imperialism became a blood-thirsty monster, and carved out large limbs of the motherland on our East and West. It is in the living memory of this ruling class that Islamic imperialism "cleaned up" its separate state of Pakistan from the "curse" of Hindu infidels. And it is under the very nose of this ruling class that Islamic imperialism, aided and abetted by petro-dollars, has started claiming for itself the rest of India as well, by a right of conquest in the past.

Islamic imperialism has only to dispute the fact that India is a Hindu homeland, and that the age-old Hindu society constitutes the core of the Indian nation with which non-Hindu communities should get integrated.

Our ruling class of secularists and socialists immediately starts seeing Hindu society as a heterogenous mass *divided* by race, religion, sect, caste, class, language, dress, food habits, local traditions, manners and mores, and what not, and *united* by nothing better than a shared slavery under the erstwhile British rulers!

It is of no avail to tell this ruling class that the British rulers were acutely aware of a deeper unity informing the vast and variegated fabric of Hindu society. It is not convinced by any amount of evidence that the British rulers did all in their power to undermine that unity in pursuance of their imperialist interests.

This ruling class has inherited many things from its British mentors. It has inherited the British state system in which the "natives" who do not know the English language and the modern Western lore, have no say. It has inherited the British style of high-living which sets it apart from the "seething mass of poor and illiterate humanity". It has inherited the British psychology of paternalism which persuades it that it alone knows what is good for the "common man". Above all, it has inherited the British "moral responsibility" for protecting the "Muslim minority". The only thing it has managed not to inherit is the British awareness of a deeper unity which holds the Hindu society together.

It is, therefore, logical for this ruling class to assert, rather aggressively, that Hindus have never been a nation. It is also logical for this ruling class to proclaim that it is too late in the day for Hindus to become, even try to become, a nation. India, we are told, is now a land of many races, religions, and cultures. The best that can be done under the circumstances, they say, is that India evolves a "secular nationalism" based on a "composite culture". The ruling class is prepared to preside over the birth-pangs of such a nationalism. The exercise is eulogised as "national integration".

It is significant that harangues for "national integration" become hectic, almost hysterical, in the wake of every street riot staged by Muslims. Our ruling class immediately starts hurling long-winded sermons on Hindus — stop being communal killers of a helpless minority; get rid of this big-brother behaviour; protect the lives and properties of your younger brethren; respect the religious and cultural rights of Muslims; and so on.

This ruling class never waits for the findings of enquiry commissions it has itself appointed to look into the causes of earlier communal riots. It does not remember or manages to forget the findings of many enquiry commissions which held that almost all riots were started by Muslims.

Hindus are expected to listen to these lectures from the ruling class with bowed heads, and with an orgy of moral self-reproach. Woe betide the irreverent Hindu who questions the legitimacy of these lectures, or who cites the evidence of enquiry commissions. He is not only a "Hindu communalist" and a "Hindu chauvinist" but also a "reactionary" and a "revivalist", putting the future of "secular and democratic India" in jeopardy. The ruling class is joined in this chorus by some pious people like the Gandhians according to whom such an unrepentant Hindu is not a Hindu at all. There is a lot of tongue-clicking all around.

In plain and simple language, therefore, national integration has come to mean only one thing, namely, that a meek Hindu society should get integrated with a militant Muslim *millat*. One waits in vain for a voice which so much as whispers a why in the face of boisterous Muslim bigotry. Muslims have a god-given right to go on raising accusing fingers at the Hindus for refusing to give them this or that. And the Hindus have a god-given duty to go on conceding every exclusive and imperialist claim of an incurable fanaticism.

The results of this "national integration" patronised by our ruling class over the past many years are there for every one to see, except, of course, its authors who are under an ideological compulsion not to see them. Caste which was for ages the most cohesive factor and a sure source of strength for Hindu society, has been converted into a cancer which poisons the very springs of our politics. Regionalism fostered by local patriotism, missionary machinations, and sectarian separatism has assumed alarming proportions such as imperil the very unity of the motherland. And Islamic imperialism has become many times more self-confident and self-righteous than on the eve of Partition.

THE CHARACTER OF HINDU UNITY

The only stumbling block which has so far stood in the way of the "national integration" promoted by our ruling class is the spirit of unity that still survives in Hindu society.

It is quite some time that Hindus lost the consciousness of their spiritual centre which unites their society, culture, and way of life. The only source of Hindu unity now is a consciousness of common history, particularly the history of freedom struggles fought against Islamic and British imperialism.

Hindu society still takes pride in its great past when it made major contributions to the spiritual, cultural, philosophical, and scientific wealth of Man. Hindu society still cherishes the memory of its great sages, seers, saints, scientists, scholars, soldiers, and statesmen. Hindu society still remembers the days of its distress when it had to struggle ceaselessly and very hard against horde after of horde Islamic invaders who not only slaughtered, burnt, pillaged, and enslaved but also tried too foist by force its own brand of barbarism.

It is this common consciousness of its history which prevents Hindu society from accepting the Mamluks, the Khaljis, the Tughlaqs, the Bahmanis, the Sharqis, the Sayyids, the Lodis, and the Mughals as native dynasties on par with the Mauryas, the Sungas, the Guptas, the Cholas, the Maukharis, the Pandyas, the Palas, the Rashtrakutas, the Yadavas, the Kakatiyas, the Hoysalas, the Sangamas, the Saluvas, the Marathas, the Sikhs, and the Jats. Hindu society can never concede that Jaypala Shahiya of Kabul, Maharani Nayakidevi of Gujarat, Prithiviraj Chauhan of Delhi, Jayachandra Gahadvad of Kanauj, Singhanadeva of Devagiri, Vikrama Pandya of Madura, Prolaya Nayak of Andhra, Harihar and Bukka and Krishnadevaraya of Vijayanagar, Maharanas Kumbha and Sanga and Pratap, Shivji, Banda Bahadur, Maharajas Surajmal and Ranjit Singh, who resisted the Islamic invaders, were petty local chieftains conspiring for personal gains. Hindu society honours these heroes as freedom fighters against Islamic imperialism, in the same way as it honours its freedom fighters against British imperialism.

THE CHARACTER OF ISLAMIC IMPERIALISM

That is what causes no end of trouble for our promoters of "national integration". The Muslim component of the "composite nation" has serious objections to this Hindu view of history and hero-worship. Muslim Indians are not at all prepared to take pride in any period of pre-Islamic Indian history, or honour any hero who flourished in that period. They want the pre-Islamic period of Indian history to be disowned even by Hindus as an "era of darkness". This, they swear, is demanded by the scriptures of Islam. But, at the same time, they want Hindus to honour criminals, gangsters, mass murderers, criminals and tyrants like Muhammad bin Qasim, Mahmud Ghaznavi, Muhammad Ghuri, Alauddin Khalji, Muhammad Tughlaq, Sikandar Lodi, Babur, Aurangzeb, and Ahmad Shah Abdali. They also expect the Hindus to denounce as disgruntled rebels, if not as traitors, the medieval Hindu heroes who resisted and ultimately routed Islamic imperialism in India.

Coming nearer to our own times, Muslim Indians are not prepared to honour Hindu rebels and revolutionaries who fought for freedom against British imperialism. They denounce as "show-boys" of the Hindus those few Muslims who cooperated with the freedom fighters. But they insist that Hindus should honour as freedom fighters the revivalists of Islamic imperialism such as Shah Walliullah and Syed Ahmad Barelvi, or separatists like Sir Syed Ahmed Khan and the Ali Brothers, or murderers of Hindus like the Wahhabis and the Moplahs, or secessionists like Mohammed Ali Jinnah.

In the field of culture, Muslim Indians harbour only a feeling of indifference, if not of contempt, for the Sanskrit, Prakrit, and Vernacular literature of ancient and medieval India. They have no use for Indian philosophies and sciences even when a lot of their own Islamic lore is borrowed from these sources and only dressed up in Arabic or Persian. They denounce Hindu spiritual traditions as polytheism and pantheism. They show no appreciation for Hindu masterpieces of architecture, sculpture, and other plastic arts. It is only in the field of music that they have shown some appreciation, simply because there has never been any Islamic music as such and many Indian musicians happen to be converts from Hinduism to Islam. The more orthodox Muslims frown even on this Muslim fondness for Hindu music.

But when it comes to what they regard as Muslim culture, they want Hindus to be as enthusiastic about it as they are themselves. They want Hindus to raise a non-stop *wah-wah* to the "wealth" of Persian and Urdu poetry, and accept as national heritage even the compositions of a Hindu-hater like Amir Khusru and a promoter of Pakistan such as Sir Muhammad Iqbal. They want Hindus to go into raptures over the beauties of Muslim architecture, miniature painting, calligraphy, culinary arts, dress, demeanour, and what not. They insist that Hindus should hail all this Islamic heritage as an inseparable part of the national heritage.

THE NATURE OF NATIONAL INTEGRATION

Our ruling class cannot see any justice in the Hindu consciousness of its pre-Islamic past, nor any injustice in the Muslim insistence on glorifying an inglorious interregnum in India's long history. The only way which this ruling class sees out of what it calls "the communal strife" is that Hindu history should be substantially diluted and tailored to the needs of Islamic imperialism, and that Muslim history should be given a liberal coat of whitewash or even made to pass muster as national history. This has been the main plank in the platform for "national integration".

Hitherto this *Experiment with Untruth* was confined mainly to Muslim and Communist "historians" who have come to control the Indian History Congress, the Indian Council of Historical Research, and even the University Grants Commission. Now it has been taken up by the National Integration Council. The Ministry of Education of the Government of India has directed the education departments in the States to extend this experiment to school-level text-books of history. And this perverse programme of suppressing truth and spreading falsehood is being sponsored by a state which inscribes *Satyameva Jayate* on its emblem.

Mrs. Coomi Kapoor has given a summary of the guidelines prepared by the National Council of Educational Research and Training (NCERT) in the *Indian Express* date-lined New Delhi, January 17, 1982. She writes: "History and Language textbooks for schools all over India will soon be revised radically. In collaboration with various state governments the Ministry of Education has begun a phased programme to weed out undesirable textbooks and remove matter which is prejudicial to national integration and unity and which does not promote social cohesion. The Ministry of Education's decision to re-evaluate textbooks was taken in the light of the recommendations of the National Integration Council of which the Prime Minister is Chairman. The Ministry's view was that history had often been used to serve narrow sectarian and chauvinistic ends." Accordingly, "Twenty states and three Union Territories have started the work of evaluation according to guidelines prepared by the NCERT. In September (1981), two evaluators from each state attended a course at NCERT headquarters in New Delhi. The evaluators are now scrutinising the relevant texts in their home states and submitting their reports. The evaluations will be examined by an expert committee appointed by the state."

We shall examine and evaluate the guidelines laid down by the NCERT in the chapters that follow.

Chapter II

THE CHARACTER OF MUSLIM RULE IN INDIA

Some of the guidelines seem to be good. It is eminently desirable that "the ancient period of Indian history cannot be referred to as the Hindu period and the medieval period as the Muslim period". It follows, though it is not mentioned in the guidelines reported by the *Indian Express,* that the modern period of Indian history also will not be named as the British period. This scheme of periodization, however, was given up by most historians quite some time ago. One only wonders what the votaries of Islamic imperialism will do without a Muslim period of Indian history.

It is also commendable that "the term Aryan cannot be used as a racial category". The term has never been used in a racial sense anywhere in the vast compendium of Indian literature. In the whole of the Rigveda the word *"Arya"* occurs only 33 times. It is in the Buddhist and Jain canons that it acquires a very wide currency, which is continued in later Sanskrit literature. But in every instance, it stands for whatever is regarded as eminent or noble. The term was used in a racial sense for the first time by Western historians who cooked up the theory of an Aryan invasion of India around 1500 BC. They also popularised, in a racial sense, the term "Dravidian" which had only a geographical connotation in the Indian tradition.

It is, however, not at all clear if the guidelines have proposed to eschew altogether the theory of an Aryan invasion of India. The only inference which can be drawn from what the guidelines state in the next breath, is that this baseless theory is not to be given up. Otherwise, it does not make sense to lay down that "historians have been told to stress the interaction between Aryan and non-Aryan cultures". The division of ancient Indian culture into Aryan and non-Aryan is itself derived from the theory of an Aryan invasion. So long as we continue to talk of Aryan and non-Aryan cultures, the terms "Aryan" and "Dravidian" cannot be divested of racial connotations.

But that is about all that can be said in commendation of the scheme sanctioned by the National Integration Council and sponsored by the Ministry of Education. The rest is recommendations for telling lies to our children, or for not telling to them the truth at all.

DECIMATION OF HINDU HERITAGE

Take for instance "the warning against over-reliance on and use of myths as history". The blow is aimed at the Ramayana and the Mahabharata and the two Hindu heroes par excellence — Sri Rama and Sri Krishna. No serious historian has ever held that the two great epics are history *per se*. But no serious historian now doubts that the epics contain a core of authentic history. The same holds good for several other myths and legends from the Puranas which all serious historians now search for genuine historical material. One wonders what harm these noble stories can do to "national integration". Hindus have been sustained by these stories for ages past. What has happened now that their children are to be deprived of this spiritual fare? The only explanation is that Islamic imperialism cannot stomach these superb stories. They cast an unfavourable reflection on whatever "heroes" Islam has had in its blood-soaked history.

But the guidelines do not stop at "mythology" alone. They invade the realm of recorded history as well. The general recommendation is summed up in a single sentence — "over-glorification of the country's past is forbidden." The specific instance is also provided immediately — "the Gupta Age can no longer be referred to as the golden period of Hinduism."

One may very well ask the champions of "national integration" as to why Hindus shouldn't glorify their ancient past, and take pride in the golden age of the Guptas? The ancient past of India is so great that it simply cannot be over-glorified. And the Gupta Age was in fact the golden age of Hindu history when Hindu spirituality, art, literature, science, and philosophy attained an acme which has not since been surpassed. Every nation has glorified one period or the other of its past history. The Chinese have their Ming period, the Persians their Age of Cyrus the Great, the Greeks their Age of Pericles, the Romans their

Age of Augustus, the Arabs their Age of the Abbasids, the English their Age of Elizabeth, the French their Age of Reason and Revolution, the Germans their Age of Bismarck, and so on. A period of greatness in which a people can take pride, provides a point of self-identification to that people. The soul of a nation is nourished by legitimate pride in a period when its creativity attained a pinnacle. Hindus can be prevented from taking pride in the Gupta Age only for very perverse reasons. The whole prescription for "national integration", therefore, cannot but become suspect in the eyes of Hindus.

The suspicion grows deeper when the guidelines move from the ancient to the medieval period of Indian history. It is recommended that "Muslim rulers cannot be identified as foreigners except for early invaders who did not settle here". We assume that what is meant by "early invaders" is early Muslim invaders and not the Greeks, the Sakas, the Kushanas, and the Hunas some of whom were rulers but not Muslims. The distinction, therefore, hinges on what is meant by "here" where the early Muslim invaders did not settle. This is a question of facts and not of interpretation. What are the facts?

The earliest Muslim invaders were the Arabs who succeeded in occupying Sindh in the second decade of the 8th century. But the Arabs did settle down in Sindh although they were constantly threatened by Hindu kings from the interior. They continued to rule over Sindh and even Multan till they were ousted from power by the Turks under Muhammad Ghuri. The very fact that the Sindhi language is still written in the Arabic script testifies to the fact that the Arabs had settled down in Sindh, and have made their presence felt till our own times.

The second wave of Muslim invaders was that of the Turks who occupied Ghazni in 963 AD, and conquered from there not only the whole of Afghanistan but also the North-West Frontier Province and a large part of the Punjab under the leadership of Subuktigin and his son, Mahmud Ghaznavi. By the time Mahmud Ghaznavi died in 1030 AD, the Turks had settled in all these areas. Some years later, they had occupied Nagaur in Rajasthan, and settled down there as well. Lahore became the capital of the Later Ghaznavids when they were ousted from Afghanistan by the Ghurids in the last quarter of the 12th century. And they were very much there till they were overthrown by Muhammad Ghuri in 1186 AD.

The third wave of Muslim invaders was led by Muhammad Ghuri who occupied the Chauhan kingdom of Haryana, Ajmer, Aligarh, and Bayana in 1192-93 AD, and the Gahadvad kingdom of UP in 1194-95 AD. His generals had conquered South Bihar, West and North Bengal, and parts of Bundelkhand by the time he was assassinated in 1206 AD. Finally, the Shamsi dynasty was established at Delhi in 1210 AD to be followed by several Muslim dynasties at this centre as well as in several provinces all over India.

Presumably, the point of time which the guidelines have in mind is 1206 or 1210 AD when the Muslim rulers are supposed to have settled down, and become native rulers. The definition of "here" we thus obtain, therefore, excludes Sindh, Afghanistan, the North-West Frontier Province, and the Punjab beyond the Satluj. But these provinces in which the early Muslim invaders had settled and over which they ruled for long periods, were very much parts of India at the time the Islamic invasions started. The Arabs recognized them as parts of Hind. So did the Turks. The guidelines should have been more honest and stated clearly that what they mean by "here" is the area which is included in India after the Partition in 1947, and that the present-day Pakistan and Afghanistan are to be treated as foreign lands from the second decade of the 8th century onwards. Students of historical geography may protest. But the guidelines have no use for such long-forgotten facts.

One is left wondering about the place of Babur in this scheme of Indian history. If Mahmud Ghaznavi and Muhammad Ghuri are to be treated as foreign invaders simply because they launched their invasions from Afghanistan, what about Babur who also invaded India from the same place? It is true that he was not an early invader, and that he decided to settle down in India after the Battle of Khanwa in 1528 AD. But the fact remains that he came from a foreign land in terms of the definition laid down by the guidelines. There are many other confusions created by the guidelines. We need not go into them at this stage of our discussion. Suffice it to say that the guidelines are wholly arbitrary in drawing a distinction between "early invaders who did not settle here", and the "Muslim rulers" who did.

One may very well ask as to why the establishment of Muslim rule at Delhi should sound so decisive for converting foreigners into natives. In 1210 AD, Delhi was not even a metropolitan city. It was comparatively a small town governed by a satrap of the Chauhans of Ajmer. Kanauj and Varanasi in U.P., Anhilwar Patan in Gujarat, Devagiri in Maharashtra, Dvarasamudra in Karnataka, Madurai in Tamil Nadu, Warrangal in Andhra Pradesh, Jajpur in Orissa, Navadvip in Bengal, Udandapur in Bihar, and Tripuri, Ujjain and Kalanjar in Madhya Pradesh, were much bigger cities and far more important as metropolitan seats of political power. Why not start converting foreign invaders into native rulers from the dates on which these cites came under Muslim occupation? Delhi started becoming important only after it became the seat of the first sultanate. Why should the future glory of Delhi get projected into the past, and be made to demarcate a decisive date in India's history? And why should Multan, Brahmanabad, Ghazni, Kabul, Peshawar, and Lahore, which were bigger and more important than Delhi at the time of their first Muslim occupation, be deprived of that honour simply because they happen to be situated in areas which are regarded as foreign at present?

Finally, one is left marvelling at the one criterion chosen by the guidelines for converting foreign invaders into natives, imperialists into patriots. One has only to settle down in India in order to become an Indian even if the settler continues to despise everything Indian and admire everything Arabic and Persian and Turkish, even if the settler continues to massacre in cold blood millions of Indians and converting many more by force and fraud, even if the settler continues to capture and sell into slavery and concubinage all over the Islamic world millions of Indian males and females, even if the settler destroys on a large scale the great creations of Indian art and science and literature, and even if the settler reduces the Indians themselves to the status of non-citizens in their own ancestral homeland.

No doubt the guidelines have in view the fact that the British rulers who came later and who are rightly regarded as foreign rulers, had a homeland to which they carried the loot from India and to which they returned in the long run. This looks like a significant fact at first glance. But it loses meaning as soon as we start looking for a homeland in the case of the Turks. We find that long before the Turks invaded India, they had lost their original homeland east of the Jaxartes, and become warrior vagabonds. They invaded Transoxiana, Sinkiang, Khurasan, and northern parts of Iran along the Caspian Sea, massacred some of the local population and intermarried with the rest, and made all these lands into their permanent homelands. Later on, they did the same in what is now known as Turkey. They tried to do the some in India but failed in the face of stiff and continued Hindu resistance. But that is a different story. What is relevant in the present context is that Muslim chroniclers of medieval India give no hint that the Turkish invaders of India ever thought of a homeland to which they could carry the loot or go back. They had come here to create another homeland for themselves.

As regards carrying the loot, what difference does it make as to where it is carried so long as looting the conquered population remains a primary occupation of the conqueror? If Mahmud Ghaznavi and Muhammad Ghuri are to be treated as foreign invaders because they carried the loot from North India to Ghazni, why not extend the logic to the Mamluks, the Khaljis, the Tughlaqs, the Lodis, the Surs, and the Mughals who brought the loot to Delhi from many other parts of India? The same logic should be applied to provincial Muslim dynasties who took the loot to Jaunpur, to Gaur and Pandua, to Dhar and Mandu, to Patan and Ahmedabad, to Daulatabad and Bidar and Gulbarga, and to Ahmadnagar and Bijapur and Golconda. And what about the Arabs in Sindh who lost contact with Arabia after the 8th century, and who retained the loot in Sindh rather than take it to their homeland? They should not be treated as early and foreign invaders if keeping the loot within India is the litmus test.

In any case, who can say that the British invaders did not settle down in India the same way as the Turks had done? Look at the splendid mansions, chapels, churches, hill stations, and big metropolitan cities including New Delhi which the British built for themselves. Look at the giant enterprises, industrial and commercial, they floated for themselves in India. There is no dearth of families in Great Britain even today who take immense pride in their Indian connection. And the British loved India as the brightest jewel in the British crown. The fact that they had a homeland to which they returned when they were forced to leave, does not really make much difference in the context of foreign invasion and rule, except for the NCERT experts who specialise in making molehills of mountains, and vice versa.

It is no use fighting the fact that Muslim rule in India was an earlier prototype of the succeeding British rule. No Muslim ruler worth his salt ever condescended to learn or speak an Indian language, except in the last days when Muslim power had collapsed. The pride of place was always given to Arabic, and Persian, and even Turkish, as to English during the British days. All positions of power and privilege were always reserved for Muslims of Arabic, or Turkish, or Persian, or even Abyssianian descent, as they were for the white men of British, or European descent later on. Every Muslim adventurer coming from Arabia, or Persia, or Khurasan, or Central Asia, or far-off North Africa and Abyssinia, could immediately obtain a position of privilege in the Muslim aristocracy, no matter how uncouth or unlettered he happened to be, as any European adventurer irrespective of his qualifications could join the exclusive Western club during the British regime. The dresses the Muslim rulers donned, the foods and drinks they relished, the pastimes they preferred, the male and female beauties they prized, the mores and manners they observed — in short, their whole life-style had as little of the Indian in it as the life-style of the latter-day British.

In fact , in several respects the British rulers were kinder to India and the Indians as compared to the medieval Muslim rulers. All Muslim rulers converted Hindus by force, demolished Hindu temples, and heaped insult and injury on every Hindu sentiment and institution. All mullahs and sufis poured ridicule and contempt on Hindu religion and culture without any compunction. But a Hindu ran the risk of his life if he so much as whispered a doubt about the exclusive claims of Islam, or the legitimacy of Islamic laws. On the other hand, the British rulers, though they encouraged Christian missionaries, never permitted them to convert Hindus by force. They never desecrated Hindu places of worship, or hurled insults at Hindu religion and culture. Their Hindu subjects could question the exclusive claims of Christianity in the open market place without inviting so much as a frown from most of the British administrators.

Another litmus test is the matter of marriages between the rulers and the ruled. Every Muslim ruler and noble thought it his right to force into his harem as many Hindu women as he fancied. He could keep Hindu concubines without any count. But a Hindu could not even dream of marrying a Muslim girl, not even a girl from a native family converted to Islam. The offence of falling in love with a Muslim woman, even a woman belonging to the family of a Hindu convert, invited capital punishment. This was never true during the British rule. They did not molest Indian women at will. They frowned at but never prevented Indians from marrying British girls.

No, the Muslim rulers of India cannot be regarded as native rulers simply because they settled down here, or because the descendants of a large number of Hindus who were converted to Islam by force now regard themselves as the descendants of those Muslim rulers and demand a gross distortion of Indian history. The Christians in India whose forefathers went over to the religion of the British rulers, may also very well advance the same argument and object to the British being regarded as foreign rulers. It is good of the Christians that so far they have not raised such a demand. But if they do, are we prepared to concede it? Appeasement of a militant *millat* may be profitable politics. But political convenience cannot dictate the definition of good history.

HEROES AND VILLAINS

It is not at all surprising that the corollaries of these controversial guidelines should be equally questionable. We are told that "Aurangzeb can no longer be referred to as the champion of Islam", and that "Shivaji cannot be overglorified in Maharashtra textbooks".

Shivaji first. It is sheer mischief to suggest that Shivaji is glorified in Maharashtra alone. The fortunate fact is that he is honoured by every Hindu worth his name, wherever that Hindu may reside in the length and breadth of India. Rabindranath Tagore, who was not a Maharashtrian, paid his homage to Shivaji in a long poem pulsating with the great poet's image of a Hindu hero. Many more poems and dramas and novels about Shivaji's chivalry and heroism are to be found in all Indian languages. It is, therefore, presumptuous on the part of some very small people to lay down that Shivaji shall not be overglorified. The fact is that he *cannot* be overglorified, such is the majesty of his character and role. The historian who will do full justice to the personality of Shivaji as well as to his role in Indian history is yet to be born. Some puny politicians pretending to be historians are trying to cut Shivaji to their own size. They are like street urchins spitting at the sun.

As regards Aurangzeb, our secularists may very well find it inconvenient to project his image as a champion of Islam. For that image, in turn, provides an image of Islam as well. And that image of Islam is far from flattering. If that image of Islam is not shielded from public gaze, it becomes difficult for our secularists to project and protect the claims of Islam as religion and culture. Human history, however, abounds in facts which are not at all flattering. These facts cannot be abolished or wished away simply because some people do not like or cannot face them. Aurangzeb is such a fact. Stalin is another. And Hitler yet another. To say that Aurangzeb was not a champion of Islam is tantamount to saying that Stalin was not a Communist and Hitler not a Nazi. And the Islam which was not championed by Aurangzeb, can be found neither in the Quran nor in the Sunnah of the Prophet. It is a figment of the secularist imagination. On the other hand, many histories written by custodians of Islam in medieval and modern times hail him as a great champion of Islam. Many mosques built over and with the debris of deliberately demolished Hindu temples stand in different parts of India as monuments to Aurangzeb's Islamic majesty.

The whole tenor of this tendentious scheme for "national integration" becomes fully explicit in the following fiat from the Ministry of Education: "Characterisation of the medieval period as a dark period or as a time of conflict between Hindus and Muslims is forbidden. Historians cannot identify Muslims as rulers and Hindus as subjects. The state cannot be described as a theocracy, without examining the actual influence of religion. No exaggeration of the role of religion in political conflicts is permitted.... Nor should there be neglect and omission of trends and processes of assimilation and synthesis."

There can, of course, be two opinions about whether the medieval period of Indian history, that is, India under Muslim rule, was a dark or dazzling period. It all depends upon how one looks upon it.

Looked at from the point of view of Islam, it was a dazzling period indeed. Islam acquired an empire over a large country full of unrivalled riches. Islam had the immense satisfaction of 1) sending millions of accursed *kāfirs* to hell in a continuous *jihād,* 2) demolishing and desecrating thousands of idolatrous places of worship and pilgrimage, 3) killing thousands of Brahmins and Bhikshus and forcing the rest to eat beef, 4) collecting vast amounts of booty and distributing it among the *mu'mins* according to rules laid down by the Prophet, 5) capturing millions of men and women and children and selling them into slavery and concubinage in the far-flung Islamic world, 6) usurping power and privilege over a vast population which was reduced to serfdom, and 7) proving the superiority of Islamic scriptures by the power of the sword.

The Muslim rulers built for themselves many sumptuous palaces full of pomp and luxury. They also built many mosques and *madrasahs,* and patronized any number of mullahs for maintaining the *millat* in spiritual health. They got themselves as well as their selected spouses buried in big *maqbaras* studded with precious stones and surrounded by well-laid gardens. They built and endowed many *khānqahs* and *dargahs* in which the sufis stayed and sang and danced and sermonised. All these monuments are now described and discussed in detail in many histories of Indo-Muslim architecture, and are photographed by an endless stream of tourists. They do leave an impression that medieval India under Muslim rule was a many-splendoured land.

Add to this architectural wealth many other arts and crafts, costumes and coiffures, calligraphy and illustrated manuscripts, Persian poetry and prose, Arabic commentaries on the Quran and the Hadis, court styles of music and dance, and *malfūzāts* of sufis and saints of Islam. Collected together in an exhibition of Islamic heritage in India, they do leave an impression that medieval India under Muslim rule was a veritable paradise of peace and prosperity.

But so far as the Hindus are concerned, this period was a prolonged spell of darkness which ended only when the Marathas and the Jats and the Sikhs broke the back of Islamic imperialism in the middle of the 18th century. The situation of the Hindus under Muslim rule is summed up by the author of *Tārīkh-i-Wassāf* in the following words: "The vein of the zeal of religion beat high for the subjection of infidelity and destruction of idols...The Mohammadan forces began to kill and slaughter, on the right and the left unmercifully, throughout the impure land, for the sake of Islām, and blood flowed in torrents. They plundered gold and silver to an extent greater than can be conceived, and an immense number of precious stones as well as a great variety of cloths... They took captive a great number of handsome and elegant maidens and children of both sexes, more than pen can enumerate... In short, the Mohammadan army brought the country to utter ruin and destroyed the lives of the inhabitants and plundered the cities, and captured their off-springs, so that many temples were deserted and the idols were broken and trodden under foot, the largest of which was Somnāt. The fragments were conveyed to Dehlī and the entrance of the Jāmi' Masjid was paved with them so that people might remember and talk of this brilliant victory... Praise be to Allah, the lord of the worlds."

Hindus cannot and should not be hoodwinked by a parade of Islamic heritage which prospered in direct proportion to their own degradation, distress, desolation, and death. It is adding insult to injury.

CHAPTER III

PLEA FOR A PERSPECTIVE

Let us now consider the next guideline from the NCERT, namely, that "characterisation of the medieval period as a time of conflict between Hindus and Muslims is forbidden".

The underlying assumption is that Muslims invaders of India in the medieval period were as good natives and patriots as the Hindus who resisted them, and that the numerous wars which the Hindus were forced to fight with the Muslim marauders were nothing more than domestic discords.

Those who have read the "histories" of this period written by the Aligarh school of "historians" and their Communist cohorts, are familiar with the arguments advanced in support of this proposition.

FACILE FORMULATION

First of all, there is the point that the Muslim invaders had settled down in India, and were no more foreigners. We have already dealt with this point in the preceding chapter.

Secondly, we are told that Hindu rajas were fighting not only with Muslim monarchs but also with other Hindu rajas. On the other hand, Muslim monarchs were frequently at war not only with Hindu rajas but also with other Muslim monarchs.

Thirdly, several instances are cited when Hindu rajas allied themselves with Muslim monarchs to fight with other Hindu rajas, and when Muslim monarchs sought and secured the help of Hindu rajas to wage wars against other Muslim monarchs.

And at the end of it all, we are invited to draw the "logical conclusion" that both Hindu and Muslim rulers were similarly and simultaneously struggling for self-aggrandisement, and that no distinction regarding their motives or missions need be drawn.

The facile nature of such formulations becomes evident as soon as we draw a parallel between what happened during the medieval period, and what happened when the British imperialists were busy building an Indian empire for themselves.

The British appeared on the scene in the first quarter of the eighteenth century. The Mughal empire at that time had started heading towards disintegration into a number of provincial principalities. The Rajputs were recovering their independence and initiative. The Marathas, the Sikhs, and the Jats were looming large on the political horizon.

The British were not the only aliens casting covetous eyes on this country. The Portuguese and the Dutch who had been worsted by the French and the British, were still hopeful of having yet another innings. The French were competing with the British on more or less equal terms for quite some time in South India. In the north-west, Nadir Shah and Ahmad Shah Abdali from neighbouring Persia and Afghanistan had also joined the fray in an effort to salvage the sinking Islamic empire for themselves.

On a superficial view, it was a free for all in which every participant was fighting simultaneously on several fronts, and seeking alliances simultaneously in several quarters. Muslims were fighting with Muslims and seeking allies among non-Muslims. Marathas were fighting with Marathas and calling on non-Marathas for help. So also the Rajputs, and the Sikhs, and the Jats. And all of them were fighting with the British, singly or in combinations which cut across demarcations of creed and community. The British themselves were fighting with the Dutch and the French on the one hand, and with the native powers on the other. They were also cooperating, now with this native power and now with that. The permutations and combinations of combat and cooperation among various powers, foreign and native, in the long-drawn-out drama from the middle of the 18th century to the middle of the 19th were such as could not be easily sorted out.

Shall we characterise this period as a period of domestic discord in which the British provided only one of the parameters? The NCERT " historians" will be the first to throw up their hands in holy horror at this mix-up of natives and foreigners, patriots and imperialists. They will be the first to advise us to have a proper perspective before we start sorting out the jigsaw puzzle.

THE PROPER PERSPECTIVE

What is the proper perspective? Looking at the history and character of various forces in the field, it should be as follows:

1. The Mughal empire, an alien imposition on India, was heading towards the dustbin of history;

2. The Rajputs, the Marathas, the Sikhs, and the Jats were rising up to reclaim their lost patrimony in their own homeland.

3. The provincial Muslim chieftains were fighting a rearguard action in order to salvage some pieces of the Mughal empire for themselves;

4. The Muslim chieftains were inviting other Islamic imperialists from across the border to come and rescue the earlier Islamic imperialists out of the morass;

5. The British, the French, and other foreign powers were trying to fish in troubled waters, and taking advantage of the ineptitude of the native and Muslim princes in order to secure their own strangleholds.

It is in this perspective that we pass a harsh judgement on the Marathas for losing the battle to the British, and allowing India to pass under another imperialist yoke. For, at that time the Marathas were the only power in the field with a potential to win national freedom from Islamic imperialism, and save India from British imperialism.

Why should we fight shy of having the same sort of proper perspective on the multifaced strife in medieval India? That strife also can be sorted out as follows:

1. On the eve of the Islamic invasion, India was witnessing a number of Hindu princes fighting among themselves for supremacy;

2. The Islamic invaders took advantage of this situation, defeated the Hindu princes one by one, and established their own empires one after another;

3. Every Islamic empire was worn out by renewed Hindu resistance, and veered on the verge of collapse;

4. A new Islamic invader intervened every time, and preserved the continuity of Islamic imperialism till British imperial-

ism appeared on the scene;

5. Sometimes a weakened Islamic empire invited some Hindu power to come to its help in its contest with a new Islamic invader.

The fact that the Hindu princes were fighting among themselves on the eve of the Islamic invasion as well as in its aftermath, should not be forced to mean that the Islamic invaders were not foreign imperialists. Nor does the fact that Hindu princes sometimes joined hands with Muslim princes to resist a new Muslim marauder from abroad, convert the Muslim princes into patriots. The Hindu princes were fighting for their hearths and homes and national honour. The Muslim princes, on the other hand, were only trying to retain the imperialist power and privilege acquired by them on earlier occasions.

The only difference between the two situations — the medieval and the modern — was that, unlike the Islamic imperialists established in India, the British imperialists did not fight physically among themselves. But this is a minor and marginal difference which should not be used to demarcate Islamic imperialism from British imperialism. The Islamic imperialists too did not engage in internecine feuds whenever there was a strong central authority to control them as in the days of the Mughal empire. We have also to make allowance for a change in the character of imperialism between the time the Mamluks "settled" down in Delhi, and the time the British "liberated" the same city from the "Maratha occupation".

The mutual strife among Muslim princes over imperialist power and privilege in India, does not change the fact that for the native Hindus all of them were enemies and oppressors of the same stock. Nor does the fact that Hindu princes were at war with each other at the same time, put them on par with Islamic invaders from abroad.

It is in this perspective that we pass a harsh judgement on the Hindu princes for their failure to combine in order 1) to resist the Islamic invader when he entered India for the first time; 2) to throw him out after he had been weakened by renewed Hindu resistance; and 3) to prevent new Islamic invaders from re-enacting the devil-dance of death, dishonour, and despoliation for the Hindus.

Let us travel a little farther down the corridors of time, and have a close look at the national struggle for freedom from British imperialism. Here also we have the same mixed situation, and have to sort it out. The ranks of freedom fighters were divided into different factions at different times. We had the liberals and the constitutionalists pitted against the extremists and the agitationists at one time. Later on, we had the non-violent non-cooperators and the revolutionaries repudiating one another. Still later, we had the leftists and the rightists struggling to capture the Indian National Congress. Alongside, we had the Hindu Mahasabha which fought the British but did not share the Congress culture of appeasing Islamic imperialism. And we had the Hindu princes, some of whom were frightened by the freedom struggle and sided with the British while some others flattered the British outwardly but sympathised with and helped the national struggle secretly.

Simultaneously, the scene was confused by that jackal, the Muslim League, waiting in the wings to jump forward and claim the lion's share of whatever concessions the freedom fighters could force out of the British imperialists with whom the Muslim League cooperated whole-heartedly in the meanwhile. Another confusing factor was the Soviet fifth-column, the Communist Party of India, which criticised and ridiculed the freedom struggle for years as "bourgeois-capitalist" but which went over to the imperialist camp when the battle was joined for a final round.

How do we look at this drama in which so many characters played so many roles? Do we absolve the British of being imperialists simply because the freedom fighters were fighting among themselves? Did the British administration in India cease to be an imperialist administration simply because some Hindu princes collaborated with it? Shall we deny patriotism to the Hindu Mahasabha simply because it clashed with the Congress on a major problem? Did the Muslim League cease to be a carrion-eater and collaborator with British imperialism simply because it developed some differences with its British patrons when the latter were getting ready to depart? Did the Soviet fifth-column become a patriotic fraternity simply because it tried to foment an armed uprising against the British in India after Soviet Russia had picked up a quarrel with Britain over sharing of the spoils after the Second World War?

The answers to all these questions are crystal clear because our perspective on the freedom struggle against British imperialism has not yet been perverted. (The NCERT guidelines are now trying to pervert it).

LOGIC OF A LACK OF PERSPECTIVE

But one can well visualise a situation when Christian missionaries will have succeeded in converting a sizable part of the Hindu population in different parts of the country. The Christian converts may very well object to their co-religionists from Britain being described as imperialist invaders from abroad. The Christian converts may very well withhold their votes from whosoever refuses to accept the British rulers as native rulers like the Hindu rulers of yore. The Christian converts may also threaten to break out into violent street riots if the British rulers are not described as great and glorious benefactors of India.

We shall then have another momentous meeting of the National Integration Council which will direct the Ministry of Education to order the NCERT to evolve another set of guidelines for new textbooks of history in the new political situation. The guidelines will sound very familiar to those who have studied the current guidelines being dished out by the NCERT. They will read as follows vis-a-vis the British period of Indian history: "The British rulers cannot be identified as foreigners. The British period will not be characterised as a time of conflict between freedom fighters and foreign imperialists. The British bureaucrats cannot be identified as rulers and Indians as subjects. Economic exploitation and cultural ruination of India under the British rule shall not be over-emphasised."

The concrete characterisation of the heroes and villains of the freedom struggle will be equally interesting under the new dispensation. The freedom fighters will have to be re-drawn as petty politicians running a rat race for personal profit! Mahatma Gandhi will have to be dethroned as the Father of the Nation, and renamed as a scheming and small-minded *bania* trying to buttress the industrial empire of the Birlas! Netaji Subhash Chandra Bose will have to be turned into a traitor who conspired with the German and the Japanese fascists against the British benefactors of India! And Pandit Jawaharlal Nehru will have to be ridiculed as a Don Quixote who presided over the passing of a ridiculous resolution demanding an independence which had never suffered an eclipse!

On the other hand, Clive, Warren Hastings, Cornwallis, Wellesley, Dalhousie, and Curzon will have to be lionised as patriots par excellence who gave us Pax Brittania, who freed us from the thugs and the pindaris, who abolished social evils like *sati*, who patronised widow remarriage, and who embellished this vast land with roads, railways, canals, communications, schools, colleges, hospitals, and what not! Mohammed Ali Jinnah will have to be hailed as an angel who came forward to relieve the British of a part of the burden when the British got tired of fighting against forces of anarchy, and decided to give up! P.C. Joshi will have to be glorified as a great statesman who resisted the Congress rabble when it started sabotaging the British war effort to save India from Japanese imperialism, and who supported the demand for Pakistan when the Congress fascists could not be stopped from seizing power!

These logical implications of the new scheme sponsored by the NCERT may sound like a distant nightmare which need not paralyse us at present. But in the field of medieval Indian history we are already upto our neck in such a nightmare. The doubting Thomases are referred to Volume 5 of *A Comprehensive History of India* sponsored by the Indian History Congress and published several year ago by the People's Publishing House, New Delhi. The late lamented Mohammad Habib who edited this history of the Sultanate starts the story from the rise of Prophet Muhammad in Arabia, and deals with the Muslim rule in India as an integral part of the larger Muslim Empire spread over Asia, Africa, and

Europe. He sees it as a splendid fabric interspersed with some instances of barbarism like that of Chengiz Khan and Halaku. Coming to the year 1192 AD, he pronounces that Prithiviraj Chauhan was executed by Muhammad Ghuri for sedition! A later day historian of British imperialism in India under the new dispensation may say the same thing about Tatya Tope, the Kukas, and revolutionaries like Bhagat Singh.

If we fight shy of these logical and inescapable implications, let us keep the record straight and not temper with it in the interests of a vote-mongering politics, nor allow it to be perverted either by Islamic imperialism masquerading as Secularism, or by the Communist traitors trumpeting the "scientific" interpretation of history.

The record leaves no doubt that the medieval period under Muslim rule was a period of continuous conflict between Hindus and Muslims. The Hindus were patriots fighting for the freedom of their ancient homeland and the preservation of their cultural patrimony. The Muslims, on the other hand, were imperialist marauders inspired by a criminal creed which they were trying to impose on the Hindus by means of force.

CHAPTER IV

THE NATURE OF CONFLICT IN MEDIEVAL INDIA

Another guideline laid down by the NCERT for school-level textbooks of history exhorts that "no exaggeration of the role of religion in political conflicts is permitted".

Let us for the time being forget the fiat of the State as to what is permitted and what is forbidden while writing the new textbooks of history. Let us first find out the facts as recorded by medieval historians, and review the various interpretations of those facts.

HINDU VIEW OF THE CONFLICT

The Hindus of medieval India have not left many accounts of the numerous wars which they were forced to fight with Muslim invaders over a period of several hundred years. All we have from the medieval Hindus are some settled sentiments expressed by them in contemporary literature regarding the nature of the Muslim menace. The Hindus advance the following seven accusations against the Muslims:

1. They kill the Brahmins and the cows;
2. They violate the chastity of Hindu women;
3. They demolish temples, and desecrate the idols;
4. They cut the tuft of hair on the head (*śikhā*) and break the sacred thread (*sūtra*);
5. They circumcise people and make them eat beef, that is, convert people by force;
6. They capture people, particularly women and children, and sell them into concubinage and slavery.
7. They plunder people's properties, and set fire to whatever they cannot carry away.

In the records referring to the rise of Vijayanagara, the Marathas, and the Sikhs, the religious motive is brought into a sharper focus. These records leave us in no doubt that the defence of Hindu Dharma was uppermost in the minds of Madhava Vidyaranya, Samartha Ramdas, and Guru Teg Bahadur. The purpose for which the sword was unsheathed by Harihar and Bukka,

Shivaji and the Sikhs, becomes quite clear in many poems written in praise of these heroes by a number of Hindu poets. The purpose, we are told, was to save the cow, the Brahmin, the *sikhā,* the *sūtra,* the honour of Hindu women, and the sanctity of Hindu places of worship.

The Hindu records about pre-Islamic foreign invasions present a striking contrast. The Greeks, the Scythians, the Kushans, and the Hunas are accused by them of savagery and lust for plunder. But they are never accused of making Hindu Dharma or its outer symbols the specific targets of their attacks. We have also the accounts of these alien invaders becoming good Shaivites, and Vaishnavas, and Buddhists after their first fury was spent, and they settled down in India.

MUSLIM VIEW OF THE CONFLICT

On the other hand, many Muslim historians of medieval India have left for posterity some very detailed, many a time day-to-day, accounts of what happened during the endless encounters between Hindus and Muslims. The dominant theme in these accounts is of *mu'mins* (Muslims) martyred; of *kāfirs* (Hindu infidels) despatched to hell; of cities and citadels sacked; of citizens massacred; of Brahmins killed or forced to eat beef; of temples razed to the ground and mosques raised on their sites; of idols broken and their pieces taken to imperial headquarters for being trodden underfoot by the faithful on the steps of the main mosque; of booty captured and carried away on elephants, camels, horses, bullock carts, on the backs of sheep and goats, and even on the heads of Hindu prisoners of war; of beautiful Hindu maidens presented to the sultans and distributed among Muslim generals and nobles; of Hindu men, women and children sold into slavery in markets all over the Islamic world; and of *kāfirs* converted to the true faith at the point of the sword. The Muslim historians treat every war waged against the Hindus as a *jihād* as enjoined by the Prophet and the Pious Caliphs.

In these Muslim accounts we never notice any note of pity, or regret, or reflection over deeds of wanton cruelty and rapacity. On the contrary, the Muslim historians express extreme satisfaction and gleeful gratitude to Allah that the mission of the Prophet has been fulfilled, the light of Islam brought to an area of darkness, and idolatory wiped out. These historians go into raptures over the richness of the booty acquired for the service of the Islamic state, for distribution among the *mujahids* and the ulema and the sufis, for the promotion of Islamic learning, and for securing the seats of Islamic power.

The same Muslim historians also narrate many wars fought between Muslim princes. Significantly, here we find no dramatisation of *mu'mins* against *kāfirs*, mosques against temples, iconoclasts against idolaters, beef-eaters against Brahmins, ravishers against maidens, and captors against child and female captives of war. They only talk of treaties violated, tributes not paid, strategy and tactics employed, horses and elephants mobilised, armaments assembled, defeats suffered, victories won, and men and equipment lost in battle. In between, there are some accounts of sacks and massacres, plunder and pillage. But there is always a wail of extreme anguish about Muslims fighting and killing other Muslims, which the Prophet had strictly prohibited.

NO CONTROVERSY ON RECORDED FACTS

These are the facts of recorded history. Only a small fraction of these facts is found in Hindu records, and that too in a stray and scattered manner. The overwhelming wealth of these facts is stored in histories written by Muslim historians in a systematic manner, dynasty by dynasty, reign by reign, battle by battle. And these Muslim histories are available in manuscript form, in cold print of modern critical editions, in original as well in translations in major world languages, in archives and liberaries all over the civilised world. Collections of these histories have always been prized as priceless possessions in the palaces of Muslim aristocracy.

There can, therefore, be no serious controversy about the facts of recorded history. There may be some differences in different accounts of the same event, reign, or regime. There may be some internal contradictions in the same accout. But these are minor details which can be sorted out by critical analysis and cross-referencing.

Sharp differences arise only when we come to the interpretation of these facts, and the passing of value judgements on them. It is here that the subjective and ideological inclinations of the interpreters and evaluators come into play. It is the varying interpretations and evaluations which have raised controversies regarding the desirability or otherwise of some textbooks in India's schools and colleges. The guidelines laid down by the NCERT are also aimed at sorting out these interpretations and evaluations.

THE VARYING INTERPRETATIONS

The orthodox or fundamentalist Muslim historians, who are coming to the forefront again with the help of petro-dollars, share the satisfaction expressed by medieval Muslim historians. They approve of and applaud unashamedly the triumphant sweep of the sword of Islam over India. They have no doubt that the medieval wars between Hindus and Muslims were fought by the Hindus as *Hindus* and by the Muslims as *Muslims*. They concur that these conflicts were armed contests between Islam and infidelity. The NCERT guidelines are aware of these orthodox Muslim historians, and warn us that "there should be no over-glorification of the medieval rule" and that "the writer should not under-emphasise condemnation of bigotry, intolerance and exclusiveness".

The academic historians, who have ruled the roost since the British bureaucrats devised our system of education in the middle of the 19th century and wrote the first textbooks of Indian history, have mostly compiled, in a chronological order, the data available in the source books and evaluated it mostly with an eye to its credibility. They have seldom conceptualised or drawn clinching conclusions regarding the nature of the conflict between Hindus and Muslims in medieval India. Their moral judgements are confined mostly to minor matters such as the justification or otherwise of a twist given to a particular treaty by a particular party. Most of the time they are preoccupied with finding the reasons for the success of those who succeeded, and the factors responsible for the failure of those who failed.

Many secularists have accused the British historians of deliberately presenting Muslim rule in India in a prejudicial, even perverse manner, in order to alienate the Hindus from the Muslims in pursuance of the British policy of divide-and-rule. A sober reflection should absolve the British of that guilt. In any case, the British have departed, and the secularists have taken over. But the Hindu-Muslim problem is far from being solved. The secularists are trying to hide their failure by advancing against "Hindu communal historians" the same accusation as they once advanced against the British historians. The only fault of the British historians was that they did not try to suppress the facts of history as recorded by Muslim historians of medieval India. Most academic historians in India after independence have followed in the footsteps of the British pioneers. The new secularist fashion of branding them as Hindu communalists is nothing short of scoundrelism.

The "modernist" Muslim historians, particularly from the Aligarh Muslim University, have increasingly come forward to "correct the perspective" of the academic historians. It is significant that the Aligarh school did not try to correct the perspective in pre-partition India except for a few Communist historians like the late lamented Mohammad Habib. In his case also the Communist version of medieval history was only a clever cloak for the orthodox Muslim version. For the rest, the Aligarh historians shared the pride which Muslim fundamentalists like Hali and Iqbal and Maulana Azad took in the Muslim conquest of India, and the painful consequence it had for the Hindus. It is only after the Independence that the Aligarh school has changed its strategy.

THE ALIGARH APOLOGISTS

To start with, the Aligarh school warns us against confusing the Turkish imperialism with Islam. The Turks had become converted to Islam no doubt. But that did not mean that they had ceased to be Turks, that is, barbarians from the steppes of Central Asia. Islam could not cure the Turks of their traditional habits of cruelty in the short spell they had spent under its sway. The cruelties which the Turks committed in India should not be laid at the door of Islam. The Turks were only using Islam as a convenient cloak for doing what they did.

Secondly, the record of atrocities attributed to the Turks needs a rigorous re-examination. We should not forget that the Muslim historians of medieval India were courtiers first and foremost. They let go their imagination, and exaggerated in an unbridled manner to please their royal patrons. Suppose a hundred Hindus and a few score Muslims were killed in a combat. The court historians manipulated the count, and reported that a thousand Hindus had been despatched to hell while a few Muslims attained martyrdom. Such reports flattered the martial vanity of Muslim potentates. Again, suppose a temple had been plundered by some insubordinate Muslim soldiers purely for the sake of the treasure it contained. The court historians reported that ten temples had been razed to the ground, twice as many idols broken to pieces, and thrice as many mosques made out of the debris. Such reports flattered the iconoclastic zeal of pious Muslim princes. And so on so forth. The tall tales told by medieval Muslim historians regarding the killing of cows and Brahmins, the molestation of maidens, the capture of booty and prisoners of war, and the conversion of Hindus by force should be taken with a fistful of salt.

To buttress this belittling of Turkish (not Muslim, mind you) barbarities, we are told that if force had been used in the service of religious zeal on a scale such as reported by the medieval Muslim historians, the whole of India would have been converted to Islam under the long spell of Muslim rule. The very fact that India was still a Hindu majority country at the end of the long period of Muslim domination, should dispel all doubts that the use of force for religious purposes was an exception rather than the rule. If there was any religious contest between Hindus and Muslims, it was of an ideological character such as that between the sufi *silsilās* on the one hand and the various sects of Hinduism on the other.

The "correct perspective", therefore, would be to treat as

purely political the wars waged by some states ruled by Muslim sultans against others ruled by Hindu rajas. The Muslim sultans were interested in building their own empires, the same as the Hindu rajas had been throughout Hindu history. It should not be held against the Muslim sultans if the peculiar caste structure of Hindu society made them victorious most of the time. In the words of Mohammad Habib, the contest was between the smiritis on the one hand and the Shariat on the other.

THE COMMUNIST "HISTORIANS"

At this point, the defence of Islam is taken over by Communist "historians", and turned into a formidable offensive against Hindu society, Hindu culture, and Hindu Dharma. The Communists accuse the "Hindu communalist historians" of always meditating morbidly on a minor mote in the Muslim eye rather than take the big beam out of their own, and have a honest view of men and matters in medieval India.

The upper caste Hindus, we are told, have always oppressed, exploited, trodden under foot, and killed at will members from a large section of Hindu society, throughout the ages. Why should they shed crocodile tears if the Turks also killed a few of these unfortunate serfs under compulsion of circumstances?

The women in Hindu society, we are informed, have always been slaves who could be molested and dishonoured without arousing so much as a ripple among the Hindu ruling classes. Why be so squeamish if the Turks freed a few of these female slaves, and gave them some status in their harems?

The whole of India, we are told, has always been a vast prison-house so far as the poor people are concerned. Why raise hell if the Turks freed some of these prisoners, and took them out to see the wide world?

Were not Hindus big beef-eaters in the Vedic times, and did they not give up this wholesome food because of the priestcraft practised upon them by those goddamned Brahmins? Why fly into a hysterical fit if the Turks made some of these Brahmins revert to healthier food habits?

Was not the vast wealth which the priests had hoarded in

those "holy" temples ill-gotten in so far as it represented a lim-
itless loot of the toiling masses, and was it not lying absolutely
useless in those dark dungeons? Why make a hue and cry if the
Turks freed some of this frozen capital, and put it to some pro-
ductive use?

As regards the idols, we are told that even if they were made
of gold and studded with precious stones, they symbolised nothing better than primitive superstition and puerile priestcraft. The
Turks did a lot of good to the mental health of the Hindus by
smashing those molochs masquerading as gods.

The truth about the so-called Muslim conquest of India, they
say, is simple and straight-forward. The Turks only helped the
enslaved Hindu masses to rise in revolt against their age-old
oppressors. Islam had brought with it a message of social equality and human brotherhood which worked a miracle on Hindu
society. Look at Kabir and Nanak and Ravidas and a hundred
other Hindu reformers who took up the Muslim message in right
earnest, and struggled for a casteless and classless Indian society.

These are not exactly the words which Communist "historians" use explicitly in their presentation of medieval Muslim history. This, however, is the exact psychology which guides their
"interpretation" of events in that period. The Aligarh apologists
can heave a sigh of relief at the sight of these Communist "historians" coming to their rescue, and taking the argument to its
logical culmination. Perhaps they themselves could have never
mustered the courage shown by the Communists. Moreover,
most of the Communist "historians" being Hindus, they carry
greater credibility.

The Communist psychology of treating with contempt everything Hindu and restoring respectability to most things Muslim,
is largely shared by the socialists, the assorted secularists, and
the rest of the Hindu "intellectuals" who pride in calling themselves modern. It is this psychology which has seeped into the
ranks of those who are now out to re-write the history of India,
particularly the history of medieval India under Muslim rule. The
politicians in power also share this psychology, and are out to
manipulate it with an eye on the Muslim vote-bank.

HINDU SCHOOL OF HISTORY NEEDED

A Hindu school of historians, alas, is not yet in sight. I cannot, therefore, present a Hindu interpretation of the history of medieval India under Muslim rule. But I believe that as soon as a Hindu school of historians is born and takes up the task of interpreting medieval Indian history, it will have little reason not to agree with the medieval Muslims historians that the medieval period was largely a period of Hindu-Muslim conflict, and that religion played a dominant role in it. Its only difference with these Muslim historians will be that it will treat as villains all those who are treated as heroes by the latter, and vice versa. It will also treat the so-called triumph of Islam in medieval India as the greatest tragedy which Islam suffered in its history after the well-deserved fate it met in 15th century Spain.

CHAPTER V
ISLAM WAS THE CULPRIT

The Aligarh apologists accuse the medieval Muslim historians of exaggerating the barbarities committed by the Muslim invaders and rulers. Next, they blame on the inherent barbarism of the Turks whatever irreducible minimum of atrocities cannot be hushed out of recorded history. And they end by absolving Islam of every crime committed in its name.

My first question is: How is it that what the Prophet of Islam did in Arabia and the Arab armies in Syria, Iraq, Iran, North Africa, Sicily, Spain and Sindh, bears such close resemblance to what the Turks did in India?

The Aligarh school is never tired of telling us that Islam would have had a brighter record in India had it been brought by the Arabs instead of the "terrible" Turks. Pandit Jawaharlal Nehru has swallowed this lie, hook, line, and sinker, and relayed it to two generations of Hindu students through his best-sellers.

Here the Aligarh apologists depend upon the ignorance of the average Hindu about the history of Arab imperialism inspired by Islam ever since the city of Yathrib was converted into Medina after conversion of its pagan citizens and massacre of the Jews. Otherwise, they would not have risked smuggling in such a stupendous lie without batting an eye.

We need not travel to distant lands in order to discover the truth about Islamic imperialism as practised and perfected by the Arabs. What the Arabs did in Sindh, as soon as they entered this unfortunate province of Bharatavarsha, provides every detail of the pattern they had repeated elsewhere.

THE ARAB RECORD IN SINDH

The *Chachnāma* which is the most famous Muslim history of the Arab conquest of Sindh, describes graphically what Muhammad bin Qasim did after that "accursed Dahir" had been "despatched" while defending the fort of Rawar: "Muhammad took the fort and stayed there for two or three days. *He put six thousand fighting men, who were in the fort, to the sword and* *shot some (more) with arrows. The other dependents were taken prisoner with their wives and children...*When the number of prisoners was calculated, it was found to amount to thirty thousand persons amongst whom thirty were the daughters of the chiefs, and one of them was Rāī Dāhir's sister's daughter whose name was Jaisiya. They were sent to Hajjāj. The head of Dāhir and the fifth part of prisoners were forwarded in charge of K'ab, son of Maharak." (emphasis added).

How did Hajjāj react towards these helpless people from Sindh? The *Chachnāma* continues: "When the head of Dāhir, the women and the property all reached Hajjāj, *he prostrated himself before Allah*, offered thanks-giving and praises...Hajjāj then forwarded the head, the umbrellas, and wealth, and prisoners to Walīd the Khalifa." (emphasis added).

The behaviour of the *Amīr-ul-mu'minīn*, (commander of the faithful) was also true to type. The *Chachnāma* relates "When the Khalifa of the time had read the letter (of Hajjāj), *he praised Allah the great. He sold some of those daughters of the chiefs, and some he granted as rewards.* When he saw the daughter of Rāī Dāhir's sister he was much struck with her beauty and charms, and began to bite his finger with astonishment. Abdullah bin Abbās desired to take her, but the Khalifa said: 'O my nephew! I exceedingly admire this girl and am so enamoured of her, that I wish to keep her for myself. Nevertheless, it is better that you take her to be the mother of your children'." (emphasis added).

Meanwhile, Muhammad bin Qasim had been conspiring with some merchants of Brahmanabad and promising protection to the common people, provided they committed treason and threw open the gates of the fort in the thick of the fight. He had some doubts whether he had done the right thing. He referred the matter to Hajjāj in a letter which was sent post haste. According to *Chachnāma*, Hajjāj replied as follows: "O my cousin! I received your life-inspiring letter...*I learnt that the ways and rules you follow are confirmable to the Law (of Islam), except that you give protection to all, great and small, and make no distinction between enemy and friend. Allah says — Give no quarter to infidels but cut their throats.* Then know that this is the command of Allah the great. You should not be too ready to grant protection, because it will prolong your work. After this, give no quarter to any enemy except to those who are of rank. This is a worthy resolve, and want of dignity will not be imputed to you." (emphasis added).

So Muhammad bin Qasim carried out the command of Allah conveyed to him by Hajjaj. The *Chachnama* carries the story forward after the fall of Brahmanabad: "When the plunder and the prisoners of war were brought before Qasim and enquiries were made about every captive, it was found that Lādī, the wife of Dāhir, was in the fort with two daughters of his by other wives. Veils were put on their faces and they were delivered to a servant to keep them apart. *One fifth of all the prisoners were chosen and set aside: they were counted as amounting to twenty thousand in number, and the rest were given to the soldiers. He sat on the seat of cruelty, and put all those who had fought to the sword. It is said that about six thousand fighting men were slain, but according to some, sixteen thousand were killed."* (emphasis added).

After "peace" had thus been restored, the conqueror took the next step. The *Chachnama* records: "Muhammad bin Qāsim fixed a tax upon all subjects *according to the laws of the Prophet.* Those who embraced Islam were exempted from slavery, the tribute and poll-tax, and from those who did not change their creed a tax was exacted according to three grades." (emphasis added).

Then followed the privilege reserved for every Muslim, conqueror or convert. According to the *Chachnama*: "As the commander of the faithful, Umar, son of Khattāb, had ordered respecting the people of Shām (Syria), so did Muhammad bin Qāsim also make a rule that every (Muslim) guest should be entertained (in Hindu homes) for one day and night, but if he fell sick then for three days and nights."

Another massacre followed at Askalanda which was surrendered by the common people after the Hindu commandant had fled: "He went into the fort, *killed four thousand fighting men with his bloody sword and sent their families into slavery.*" And Multan: "*Six thousand warriors were put to death, and all their relations and dependents were taken as slaves.*" (emphasis added). The *Chachnāma* chooses a Brahmin of Multan to proclaim Muhammad bin Qāsim's momentous victory in the following words: "Heathenism is now at an end, the temples are thrown down, the world has received the light of Islam, and mosques are built instead of idols temples." The Brahmin was a new convert.

Al Biladuri who died in 892-893 AD wrote another account of the Arab conquest of Sindh. He tells us in his *Futūhul-Buldān*: "We are told that Hajjāj caused a calculation to be made of the sums expanded in fitting out this expedition of Muhammad bin Qāsim, and the riches which resulted from it. He had spent 60 million *dirhams* and that which had been sent to him amounted to 120 millions *dirhams*."

This 120 million *dirhams* represents only one-fifth of the total loot which was paid into the Caliph's coffers according to a rule laid down by the prophet of Islam. Another four hundred and eighty million *dirhams* were distributed among Muslim soldiers in the field. Again, this total of 600 million *dirhams* does not include the sale proceeds of nearly two hundred thousand Hindu men, women and children who were taken prisoners and put to auction all over the world of Islam at that time.

PERFORMANCE OF THE PATHANS

My second question is: How come that the Pathans, who hated the Turks and fought them tooth and nail throughout the medieval period, followed the Turks so faithfully in their treatment of the Hindus?

Take Sikandar Lodi. He was the son of a Pathan father. His mother was the daughter of a Hindu goldsmith of Sirhind. Abdullah records as follows in his *Tārīkh-i-Dāūdī* written in the reign of Jahangir: "It is also related of this prince that before his accession, when a crowd of Hindūs had assembled in immense numbers at Kurkhet, he wished to go to Thanesar for the purpose of putting them all to death...He was so zealous a Musalmān that he utterly destroyed diverse places of worship of the infidels and left not a vestige remaining of them. He entirely ruined the shrines of Mathura, the mine of infidelism, and turned the principal Hindū places of worship into caravanserais and colleges. Their stone images were given to the butchers to serve as meat-weights, and all the Hindūs in Mathura were strictly prohibited from shaving their heads and beards and bathing at the *ghāts.*" Badauni writes in his *Muntakhāb-ut-Tawārīkh* that "he took the fort (of Untgarh) and gave the infidels as food for the sword. He then cast down the idol temples and built there a lofty mosque." He repeated the performance at Narwar next year, and at many other places in the years that followed

BEHAVIOUR OF HINDU CONVERTS

My third question is: How do we explain the behaviour of marauders who were not Turks but Hindus converted to Islam, and who behaved no better, if not worse, than the much-maligned Turks?

The story of Kalapahar and his exploits in Bengal and Orissa may be dismissed by the Aligarh apologists as a cock-and-bull story cooked up by "Hindu old women". But the achievements of Malik Kafur are recorded by no less an authority than Amir Khusru who was also a contemporary. Malik Kafur was a handsome young Hindu who was captured and enslaved when Ulugh Khan and Nusrat Khan, two generals of Alauddin Khalji, invaded Gujarat in 1298 AD. He was bought by Nusrat Khan for a thousand *dinārs*, converted to Islam, and presented to the emperor at Delhi. Alauddin was infatuated by Kafur who rose rapidly to be the topmost officer of the empire, titled Malik Naib.

Kafur led his famous expedition to the South in 1310-1311 AD. Devagiri was already a tributary of the Delhi Sultanate. The Hoysala King of Dvarasamudra was frightened into surrender. But the Pandya prince of Madurai refused either to purchase peace or fight a pitched battle. He tired out the Malik Naib by his hit and run tactics. The Malik Naib took it out on the non-combatant common people and their temples. At Brahmastapur (modern Chidambaram), he massacred the citizens, demolished the golden temple, and dug up its foundations. Next, the temples at Srirangam and in the neighbourhood of Kannanur were sacked. At Madurai he set fire to the temple of Sokkanatha. He had to beat a retreat in the face of fierce Hindu resistance. But he did not forget to capture and carry with him an immense booty and hordes of prisoners who were sold into slavery all along his long route to the imperial headquarters at Delhi.

Or take the case of Suhabhatta, the chief minister of Sikandar Butshikan of Kashmir (1389-1413 AD). Suhabhatta who had renounced his ancestral faith for Islam is known as Suhā in the *Rājataringiṇī* of Jonarāja. This historian of Kashmir records: "Instructed by *mlechhas*, (Suhā) instigated the king to break down the images of Gods. The king forgot his kingly duties and took a delight day and night in breaking images...He broke the images of Mārtaṇḍa, Vishaya, Īśāna, Chakravaratī and Tripureśvara... There was no city, no town, no village, no wood where Suhā and the Turushka left the temples of Gods unbroken."

Suhabhatta continued to be the chief minister under Sikandar's son, Ali Shah (1413-1420 AD). During Sikandar's reign, he had stopped at destroying Hindu temples. Under the new regime, he started persecuting the Brahmins. Their religious performances and processions were banned. The traditional allowances of the Brahmins were stopped. The Brahmins, therefore, became beggars "who had to move from door to door, like dogs, for food". Many of them tried to flee the land to escape oppression and save their caste. But they could not do so without an official permit. As a result, many of them committed suicide by fire, poison, drowning, hanging, and jumping from precipices. Amidst all this, Suhabhatta maintained that he bore no malice towards the Brahmins, and that he was only doing his duty towards Islam!

TURKS WERE BRUTALISED BY ISLAM

My fourth question is: Were the Turks really such black barbarians as they have been painted by the Aligarh apologists? How then do we explain the glaring contradiction in the behaviour of many Turkish kings who were such fearsome fiends when dealing with Hindus, but who became benevolent monarchs when dealing with Muslims?

Take Mahmud Ghaznavi who tops the list of Muslim invaders most hated by Hindus. Muhammad Nazim, a "modern historian," writes as follows in his well-documented monograph, *The Life and Times of Sultan Mahmud of Ghazna:* "The Sultan was affectionate by nature... Sultan Mahmud was strict in the administration of justice... Sultan Mahmud was a poet and scholar of some reputation. He is said to have been the author of a book named *Tafridul-Furu* which was regarded as a standard work on Fiqh...The Sultan was a great patron of learning and his court was the rendezvous of scholars from all parts of the Muslim world... His meanest rewards were calculated in thousands of *dinārs,* and the later generation of poets cherished his memory chiefly as a giver of 'elephant loads' of gold and silver." Firishta records that he used the war booty captured from Kanauj for building at Ghazni a magnificent mosque, a university well-stocked with books, and a museum full of many curiosities.

Or take Jalaluddin Khalji. He was second to none among the Muslim kings when it came to heaping atrocities on Hindus. But when Malik Chhajju, who had rebelled against him and caused bloodshed, was brought before him in chains, he overruled his advisers for harsh punishment with the remark that he would rather renounce his throne than shed the blood of a Muslim! Again, when the Rana of Ranthambhor refused to surrender, Jalaluddin gave up the siege of the fort, in spite of protests from his generals, with the remark that he did not consider ten such forts worth a single hair of a Muslim's head!

Firuz Shah Tughlaq was a great patron of learning, a builder of new cities, and patron of many public works such as tanks, gardens, and canals. In his autobiography he writes: "Better a people's weal than treasures vast; better an empty chest than hearts downcast." But by "people" he meant only the Muslims. For Hindus he was nothing short of a monster.

The much-maligned Turk did have another face which was far from being that of a barbarian. It is quite another matter that the benevolent face of the Turk was always and exclusively turned towards his Muslim *Ummah*, and never towards the "accursed" Hindus. What is relevant here is that crimes committed by the Turks in India cannot be explained away in terms of a barbarism inherent in his race. Pandit Jawaharlal Nehru who also blames the crimes of Islam on the barbarism of the Turks says in the same breath that the Turks were Buddhists before they got converted to Islam. Was it Buddhism that had brutalised the Turks? Or had Buddhism failed to humanise them?

But even if we concede, for the sake of argument, that the Turk was a born barbarian, the basic question remains unanswered. Some of the medieval Muslim historians were not Turks. They were Arabs and Persians whom the Aligarh apologists credit with the quintessence of Islamic culture. Quite a few of them were learned mullahs conversant with the commandments of Islam. The positions and privileges they obtained in the courts of their Turkish patrons were entirely due to their erudition.

So my fifth and final question is: Why did these medieval Muslim historians credit their patrons with crimes which the latter had not committed, or exaggerate the scale of some minor misdemeanours?

Before we find answers to these five questions let us first have a look at the scale and magnitude of the crimes which medieval Muslim historians have laid at the doors of most of the Muslim monarchs and their minions. Let us see if the narrations of those crimes reveal a pattern. Then we shall proceed to inquire if the pattern conforms to the crudities of normal human nature, or to the commands of an inhuman and imperialist ideology masquerading as religion.

CHAPTER VI

THE MAGNITUDE OF MUSLIM ATROCITIES — I

The world famous historian, Will Durant has written in his *Story of Civilisation* that "the Mohammedan conquest of India was probably the bloodiest story in history".

India before the advent of Islamic imperialism was not exactly a zone of peace. There were plenty of wars fought by Hindu princes. But in all their wars, the Hindus had observed some time-honoured conventions sanctioned by the Śāstras. The Brahmins and the Bhikshus were never molested. The cows were never killed. The temples were never touched. The chastity of women was never violated. The non-combatants were never killed or captured. A human habitation was never attacked unless it was a fort. The civil population was never plundered. War booty was an unknown item in the calculations of conquerors. The martial classes who clashed, mostly in open spaces, had a code of honour. Sacrifice of honour for victory or material gain was deemed as worse than death.

Islamic imperialism came with a different code — the Sunnah of the Prophet. It required its warriors to fall upon the helpless civil population after a decisive victory had been won on the battlefield. It required them to sack and burn down villages and towns after the defenders had died fighting or had fled. The cows, the Brahmins, and the Bhikshus invited their special attention in mass murders of non-combatants. The temples and monasteries were their special targets in an orgy of pillage and arson. Those whom they did not kill, they captured and sold as slaves. The magnitude of the booty looted even from the bodies of the dead, was a measure of the success of a military mission. And they did all this as *mujāhids* (holy warriors) and *ghāzīs* (*kāfir*-killers) in the service of Allah and his Last Prophet.

Hindus found it very hard to understand the psychology of this new invader. For the first time in their history, Hindus were witnessing a scene which was described by *Kānhaḍade Prabandha* (1456 AD) in the following words: "The conquering army burnt villages, devastated the land, plundered people's wealth, took Brahmins and children and women of all classes captive, flogged with thongs of raw hide, carried a moving prison with it, and converted the prisoners into obsequious Turks." That was written in remembrance of Alauddin Khalji's invasion of Gujarat in the year 1298 AD. But the gruesome game had started three centuries earlier when Mahmud Ghaznavi had vowed to invade India every year in order to destroy idolatry, kill the *kāfirs*, capture prisoners of war, and plunder vast wealth for which India was well-known.

MAHMUD GHAZNAVI AND SON

In 1000 AD Mahmud defeated Raja Jaipal, a scion of the Hindu Shahiya dynasty of Kabul. This dynasty had been for long the doorkeeper of India in the Northwest. Mahmud collected 250,000 *dinārs* as indemnity. That perhaps was normal business of an empire builder. But in 1004 AD he stormed Bhatiya and plundered the place. He stayed there for some time to convert the Hindus to Islam with the help of mullahs he had brought with him. In 1008 AD he captured Nagarkot (Kangra). The loot amounted to 70,000,000 *dirhams* in coins and 700,400 *mans* of gold and silver, besides plenty of precious stones and embroidered cloths. In 1011 AD he plundered Thanesar which was undefended, destroyed many temples, and broke a large number of idols. The chief idol, that of Chakraswamin, was taken to Ghazni and thrown into the public square for defilement under the feet of the faithful. According to *Tārīkh-i-Yamīnī* of Utbi, Mahmud's secretary, "The blood of the infidels flowed so copiously [at Thanesar] that the stream was discoloured, notwithstanding its purity, and people were unable to drink it. The Sultān returned with plunder which is impossible to count. Praise he to Allah for the honour he bestows on Islām and Muslims."

In 1013 AD Mahmud advanced against Nandana where the Shahiya king, Anandapal, had established his new capital. The Hindus fought very hard but lost. Again, the temples were destroyed, and innocent citizens slaughtered. Utbi provides an account of the plunder and the prisoners of war: "The Sultān returned in the rear of immense booty, and slaves were so plentiful that they became very cheap and men of respectability in their native land were degraded by becoming slaves of common shop-keepers. But this is the goodness of Allah, who bestows honour on his own religion and degrades infidelity."

The road was now clear for an assault on the heartland of Hindustan. In December 1018 AD Mahmud crossed the Yamuna, collected 1,000,000 *dirhams* from Baran (Bulandshahar), and marched to Mahaban in Mathura district. Utbi records: "The infidels...deserted the fort and tried to cross the foaming river...but many of them were slain, taken or drowned... Nearly fifty thousand men were killed." Mathura was the next victim. Mahmud seized five gold idols weighing 89,300 *miskals* and 200 silver idols. According to Utbi, "The Sultān gave orders that all the temples should be burnt with naptha and fire, and levelled with the ground." The pillage of the city continued for 20 days.

Mahmud now turned towards Kanauj which had been the seat of several Hindu dynasties. Utbi continues: "In Kanauj there were nearly ten thousand temples... Many of the inhabitants of the place fled in consequence of witnessing the fate of their deaf and dumb idols. Those who did not fly were put to death. The Sultān gave his soldiers leave to plunder and take prisoners." The Brahmins of Munj, which was attacked next, fought to the last man after throwing their wives and children into fire. The fate of Asi was sealed when its ruler took fright and fled. According to Utbi, "the Sultān ordered that his five forts should be demolished from their foundations, the inhabitants buried in their ruins, and the soldiers of the garrison plundered, slain and captured".

Shrawa, the next important place to be invaded, met the same fate. Utbi concludes: "The Muslims paid no regard to the booty till they had satiated themselves with the slaughter of the infidels and worshippers of sun and fire. The friends of Allah searched the bodies of the slain for three days in order to obtain booty...The booty amounted in gold and silver, rubies and pearls nearly to three hundred thousand *dirhams*, and the number of prisoners may be conceived from the fact that each was sold for two to ten *dirhams*. These were afterwards taken to Ghazni and merchants came from distant cities to purchase them, so that the countries of Mawaraun-Nahr, Iraq and Khurasan were filled with them, and the fair and the dark, the rich and the poor, were commingled in one common slavery."

Mahmud's sack of Somnath is too well-known to be retold here. What needs emphasising is that the fragments of the famous Śivaliṅga were carried to Ghazni. Some of them were turned into steps of the Jama Masjid in that city. The rest were sent to Mecca, Medina, and Baghdad to be desecrated in the same manner.

Mahmud's son Masud tried to follow in the footsteps of his father. In 1037 AD he succeeded in sacking the fort of Hansi which was defended very bravely by the Hindus. The *Tārīkh-us-Subuktigīn* records: "The Brahmins and other high ranking men were slain, and their women and children were carried away captive, and all the treasure which was found was distributed among the army." Masud could not repeat the performance due to his preoccupations elsewhere.

MUHAMMAD GHURI AND HIS LIEUTENANTS

Invasion of India by Islamic imperialism was renewed by Muhmmad Ghuri in the last quarter of the 12th century. After Prithiviraj Chauhan had been defeated in 1192 AD, Ghuri took Ajmer by assault. According the *Tāj-ul-Mā'sīr* of Hasan Nizami, "While the Sultan remained at Ajmer, he destroyed the pillars and foundations of the idol temples and built in their stead mosques and colleges and precepts of Islām, and the customs of the law were divulged and established."

Next year he defeated Jayachandra of Kanauj. A general massacre, rapine, and pillage followed. The Gahadvad treasuries at Asni and Varanasi were plundered. Hasan Nizami rejoices that "in Benares which is the centre of the country of Hind, they destroyed one thousand temples and raised mosques on their foundations". According to *Kāmil-ut-Tawārīkh* of Ibn Asir, "The slaughter of Hindus (at Varanasi) was immense; none were spared except women and children, and the carnage of men went on until the earth was weary." The women and children were spared so that they could be enslaved and sold all over the Islamic world. It may be added that the Buddhist complex at Sarnath was sacked at this time, and the Bhikshus were slaughtered.

Ghuri's lieutenant Qutbuddin Aibak was also busy meanwhile. Hasan Nizami writes that after the suppression of a Hindu revolt at Kol (Aligarh) in 1193 AD, Aibak raised "three bastions as high as heaven with their heads, and their carcases became food for beasts of prey. The tract was freed from idols and idol-worship and the foundations of infidelism were destroyed." In 1194 AD Aibak destroyed 27 Hindu temples at Delhi and built the *Quwwat-ul-Islām* mosque with their debris. According to Nizami, Aibak "adorned it with the stones and gold obtained from the temples which had been demolished by elephants". In 1195 AD the Mher tribe of Ajmer rose in revolt, and the Chaulukyas of Gujarat came to their assistance. Aibak had to invite re-inforcements from Ghazni before he could meet the challenge. In 1196 AD he advanced against Anahilwar Patan, the capital of Gujarat. Nizami writes that after Raja Karan was defeated and forced to flee, "fifty thousand infidels were despatched to hell by the sword" and "more than twenty thousand slaves, and cattle beyond all calculation fell into the hands of the victors". The city was sacked, its temples demolished, and its palaces plundered. On his return to Ajmer, Aibak destroyed the Sanskrit College of Visaladeva, and laid the foundations of a mosque which came to be known as *Aḍhāī Din kā Jhoṁpaḍā*. Conquest of Kalinjar in 1202 AD was Aibak's crowning achievement. Nizami concludes: "The temples were converted into mosques... Fifty thousand men came under the collar of slavery and the plain became black as pitch with Hindus."

A free-lance adventurer, Muhammad Bakhtyar Khalji, was moving further east. In 1200 AD he sacked the undefended university town of Odantpuri in Bihar and massacred the Buddhist monks in the monasteries. In 1202 AD he took Nadiya by surprise. Badauni records in his *Muntakhāb-ut-Tawārīkh* that "property and booty beyond computation fell into the hands of the Muslims and Muhammad Bakhtyar having destroyed the places of worship and idol temples of the infidels founded mosques and Khanqahs".

THE SLAVE (MAMLUK) SULTANS

Shamsuddin Iltutmish who succeeded Aibak at Delhi invaded Malwa in 1234 AD. He destroyed an ancient temple at Vidisha. Badauni reports: "Having destroyed the idol temple of Ujjain which had been built six hundred years previously, and was called Mahakal, he levelled it to its foundations, and threw down the image of Rai Vikramajit from whom the Hindus reckon their era, and brought certain images of cast molten brass and placed them on the ground in front of the doors of mosques of old Delhi, and ordered the people of trample them under foot."

Muslim power in India suffered a serious setback after Iltutmish. Balban had to battle against a revival of Hindu power. The Katehar Rajputs of what came to be known as Rohilkhand in later history, had so far refused to submit to Islamic imperialism. Balban led an expedition across the Ganges in 1254 AD. According to Badauni, "In two days after leaving Delhi, he arrived in the midst of the territory of Katihar and put to death every male, even those of eight years of age, and bound the women." But in spite of such wanton cruelty, Muslim power continued to decline till the Khaljis revived it after 1290 AD.

THE KHALJIS

Jalaluddin Khalji led an expedition to Ranthambhor in 1291 AD. On the way he destroyed Hindu temples at Jhain. The broken idols were sent to Delhi to be spread before the gates of the Jama Masjid. His nephew Alauddin led an expedition to Vidisha in 1292 AD. According to Badauni, Alauddin "brought much booty to the Sultan and the idol which was the object of worship of the Hindus, he caused to be cast in front of the Badaun gate to be trampled upon by the people. The services of Alauddin were highly appreciated, the jagir of Oudh also was added to his other estates."

Alauddin became Sultan in 1296 AD after murdering his uncle and father-in-law, Jalaluddin. In 1298 AD he equipped an expedition to Gujarat under his generals Ulugh Khan and Nusrat Khan. In an earlier chapter I have already quoted *Tārīkh-i-Wassāf* on the "achievements" of this expedition. The invaders plundered the ports of Surat and Cambay. The temple of Somnath, which had been rebuilt by the Hindus, was plundered and the idol taken to Delhi for being trodden upon by the Muslims. The whole region was subjected to fire and sword, and Hindus were slaughtered *en masse*. Kamala Devi, the queen of Gujarat, was captured along with the royal treasury, brought to Delhi and forced into Alauddin's harem. The doings of the Malik Naib during his expedition to South India in 1310-1311 AD have already been described.

THE TUGHLAQS

Muslim power again suffered a setback after the death of Alauddin Khalji in 1316 AD. But it was soon revived by the Tughlaqs. By now most of the famous temples over the length and breadth of the Islamic empire in India had been demolished, except in Orissa and Rajasthan which had retained their independence. By now most of the rich treasuries had been plundered and shared between the Islamic state and its swordsmen. Firuz Shah Tughlaq led an expedition to Orissa in 1360 AD. He destroyed the temple of Jagannath at Puri, and desecrated many other Hindu shrines. According to *Sīrat-i-Fīrūz Shāhī* which he himself wrote or dictated, "Allah who is the only true God and has no other emanation, endowed the king of Islām with the strength to destroy this ancient shrine on the eastern sea-coast and to plunge it into the sea, and after its destruction he ordered the image of Jagannāth to be perforated, and disgraced it by casting it down on the ground. They dug out other idols which were worshipped by the polytheists in the kingdom of Jājnagar and overthrew them as they did the image of Jagannāth, for being laid in front of the mosques along the path of the Sunnis and the way of the *musallis* (Muslim congregation for *namāz*) and stretched them in front of the portals of every mosque, so that the body and sides of the images might be trampled at the time of ascent and descent, entrance and exit, by the shoes on the feet of the Muslims."

After the sack of the temples in Orissa, Firuz Shah Tughlaq attacked an island on the sea-coast where "nearly 100,000 men of Jājnagar had taken refuge with their women, children, kinsmen and relations". The swordsmen of Islam turned "the island into a basin of blood by the massacre of the unbelievers". A worse fate overtook the Hindu women. *Sīrat-i-Fīrūz Shāhī* records: "Women with babies and pregnant ladies were haltered, manacled, fettered and enchained, and pressed as slaves into service in the house of every soldier."

Still more horrible scenes were enacted by Firuz Shah Tughlaq at Nagarkot (Kangra) where he sacked the shrine of Jvalamukhi. Firishta records that the Sultan "broke the idols of Jvālāmukhī, mixed their fragments with the flesh of cows and hung them in nosebags round the necks of Brahmins. He sent the principal idol as trophy to Medina."

AMIR TIMUR

The climax came during the invasion of Timur in 1399 AD. He starts by quoting the Quran in his *Tuzk-i-Timūrī*: "O Prophet, make war upon the infidels and unbelievers, and treat them severely." He continues: "My great object in invading Hindustan had been to wage a religious war against the infidel Hindus...[so that] the army of Islam might gain something by plundering the wealth and valuables of the Hindus."

To start with he stormed the fort of Kator on the border of Kashmir. He ordered his soldiers "to kill all the men, to make prisoners of women and children, and to plunder and lay waste all their property". Next, he "directed towers to be built on the mountain of the skulls of those obstinate unbelievers". Soon after, he laid siege to Bhatnir defended by Rajputs. They surrendered after some fight, and were pardoned. But Islam did not bind Timur to keep his word given to the "unbelievers". His *Tuzk-i-Timūrī* records: "In a short space of time all the people in the fort were put to the sword, and in the course of one hour the heads of 10,000 infidels were cut off. The sword of Islam was washed in the blood of the infidels, and all the goods and effects, the treasure and the grain which for many a long year had been stored in the fort became the spoil of my soldiers. They set fire to the houses and reduced them to ashes, and they razed the buildings and the fort to the ground."

At Sarsuti, the next city to be sacked, "all these infidel Hindus were slain, their wives and children were made prisoners and their property and goods became the spoil of the victors". Timur was now moving through Haryana, the land of the Jats. He directed his soldiers to "plunder and destroy and kill every one whom they met". And so the soldiers "plundered every village, killed the men, and carried a number of Hindu prisoners, both male and female". Loni which was captured before he arrived at Delhi was predominantly a Hindu town. But some Muslim inhabitants were also taken prisoners. Timur ordered that "the Musulman prisoners should be separated and saved, but the infidels should all be despatched to hell with the proselytising sword".

By now Timur had captured 100,000 Hindus. As he prepared for battle against the Tughlaq army after crossing the Yamuna, his Amirs advised him "that on the great day of battle these 100,000 prisoners could not be left with the baggage, and that it would be entirely opposed to the rules of war to set these idolators and enemies of Islam at liberty". Therefore, "no other course remained but that of making them all food for the sword". *Tuzk-i-Timūrī* continues: "I proclaimed throughout the camp that every man who had infidel prisoners should put them to death, and whoever neglected to do so should himself be executed and his property given to the informer. When this order became known to the *ghāzīs* of Islam, they drew their swords and put their prisoners to death. One hundred thousand infidels, impious idolators, were on that day slain. Maulana Nasiruddin Umar, a counsellor and man of learning, who , in all his life, had never killed a sparrow, now, in execution of my order, slew with his sword fifteen idolatrous Hindus, who were his captives."

The Tughlaq army was defeated in the battle that ensued next day. Timur entered Delhi and learnt that a "great number of Hindus with their wives and children, and goods and valuables, had come into the city from all the country round". He directed his soldiers to seize these Hindus and their property. *Tuzk-i-Timūrī* concludes: "Many of them (Hindus) drew their swords and resisted...The flames of strife were thus lighted and spread through the whole city from Jahānpanah and Siri to Old Delhi, burning up all it reached. The Hindus set fire to their houses with their own hands, burned their wives and children in them and rushed into the fight and were killed...On that day, Thursday, and all the night of Friday, nearly 15,000 Turks were engaged in slaying, plundering and destroying. When morning broke on Friday, all my army ...went off to the city and thought of nothing but killing, plundering and making prisoners....The following day, Saturday the 17th, all passed in the same way, and the spoil was so great that each man secured from fifty to a hundred prisoners, men, women, and children. There was no man who took less than twenty. The other booty was immense in rubies, diamonds, garnets, pearls, and other gems and jewels; *ashrafis*, tankas of gold and silver of the celebrated Alāi coinage: vessels of gold and silver; and brocades and silks of great value. Gold and silver ornaments of Hindu women were obtained in such quantities as to exceed all account. Excepting the quarter of the Saiyids, the *ulama* and the other Musulmāns, the whole city was sacked."

CHAPTER VII

THE MAGNITUDE OF MUSLIM ATROCITIES — II

The NCERT is not the only villain in the game of propping up palpable falsehoods in the field of medieval Indian history. For quite some time, the All India Radio has been presenting a programme in Hindi — *Itihāsa Ke Jharokhe Se* (Window on History). The refrain is that medieval India under Muslim rule was a period of peace and amity between Hindus and Muslims, and that Muslim rulers, particularly Aurangzeb, went out of their way to be kind and considerate to the Hindus. The insinuation is that the Hindu-Muslim strife was a creation of the British imperialists whose "nefarious game" is now being continued by "Hindu communalists".

The evidence cited by the speakers in this AIR programme is always an exercise in *suppressio veri suggestio falsi*. For instance, Aurangzeb's petty donations to 2-3 Hindu temples patronized by some pet Hindu courtiers, are played up with great fanfare. But his systematic demolition of thousands of Hindu temples and defilement of countless images of Gods and Goddesses, throughout his long reign, is never mentioned. Such pitiable attempts at pitting molehills of munificence against mountains of malevolence, go against all sense of proportion in judging a whole period of Indian history. It is also a very sad spectacle of the slave mentality which was imbibed by a certain section of Hindu intelligentsia during the long spell of Islamic imperialism in India: The master has a god-given right to kick his slave a hundred times a day. But the master deserves gratitude from the slave if the former smiles on the latter once in a blue moon. It is understandable if an apologist of Islam sings the glories of the Islamic empire in India. But for a Hindu to participate in this programme is the limit of self-abasement. No amount of swearing by Secularism can cover up the sin.

One may very well ask the purveyors of this puerile propaganda that if the record of Islam in medieval India was so bright and blameless, where is the need for this daily ritual of whitewashing it. Hindu heroes like Chandragupta Maurya, Samudragupta, Harihar, Bukka, Maharana Pratap, and Shivaji, to name only a few of the notables, have never needed any face-lift. Why does the monstrous mien of an Alauddin Khalji, a Firuz Shah Tughlaq, a Sikandar Lodi, and an Aurangzeb, to name only the most notorious, pop out so soon from the thickest coat of cosmetics?

The answer is provided by the Muslim historians of medieval India. They painted their heroes in the indelible dyes of Islamic ideology. They did not anticipate the day when Islamic imperialism in India will become only a painful memory of the past. They did not visualise that the record of Islam in India will one day be weighed on the scales of human values. Now it is too late for trying to salvage Islam in medieval India from it blood-soaked history. The orthodox Muslim historians are honest when they state that the medieval Muslim monarchs were only carrying out the commandments of Islam when they massacred, captured, enslaved, and violated Hindu men, women and children; desecrated, demolished, and destroyed Hindu places of worship; and dispossessed the Hindus of all their wealth. The Aligarh "historians" and their secularist patrons are only trying to prop up imposters in place of real and living characters who played life-size roles in history.

I have already related what some of the sultans were doing to the Hindus from their imperial seat at Delhi. The provincial Muslim satraps who became independent whenever Delhi had a weak Muslim monarch, behaved no better.

THE PROVINCIAL MUSLIM SATRAPS

In 1391 AD the Muslims of Gujarat complained to Nasiruddin Muhammad, the Tughlak Sultan of Delhi, that the local governor, Farhat-ul-Mulk, was practising tolerance towards the Hindus. The Sultan immediately appointed Muzaffar Khan as the new governor. He became independent after the death of the Delhi Sultan and assumed the title of Muzaffar Shah in 1392 AD. Next year he led an expedition to Somnath and sacked the temple which the Hindus had built once again. He killed many Hindus to chastise them for this "impudence", and raised a mosque on the site of the ancient temple. The Hindus, however, restarted restoring the temple soon after. In 1401 AD Muzaffar came back with a huge army. He again killed many Hindus, demolished the temple once more, and erected another mosque. Muzaffar was succeeded by his grandson, Ahmad Shah, in 1411 AD. Three years later Ahmad appointed a special *dārogah* to destroy all temples throughout Gujarat. In 1415 AD Ahmad invaded Sidhpur where he destroyed the images in Rudramahalaya, and converted the grand temple into a mosque. Sidhpur was renamed Sayyadpur.

Mahmud Begrha who became the Sultan of Gujarat in 1458 AD was the worst fanatic of this dynasty. One of his vassals was the Mandalika of Junagadh who had never withheld the regular tribute. Yet in 1469 AD Mahmud invaded Junagadh. In reply to the Mandalika's protests, Mahmud said that he was not interested in money as much as in the spread of Islam. The Mandalika was forcibly converted to Islam and Junagadh was renamed Mustafabad. In 1472 AD Mahmud attacked Dwarka, destroyed the local temples, and plundered the city. Raja Jayasingh, the ruler of Champaner, and his minister were murdered by Mahmud in cold blood for refusing to embrace Islam after they had been defeated and their country pillaged and plundered. Champaner was renamed Mahmudabad.

Mahmud Khalji of Malwa (1436-69 AD) also destroyed Hindu temples and built mosques on their sites. He heaped many more insults on the Hindus. Ilyas Shah of Bengal (1339-1379 AD) invaded Nepal and destroyed the temple of Svayambhunath at Kathmandu. He also invaded Orissa, demolished many temples, and plundered many places. The Bahmani sultans of Gulbarga and Bidar considered it meritorious to kill a hundred thousand Hindu men, women, and children every year. They demolished and desecrated temples all over South India.

BABUR

The scene shifted once mere to Delhi after Babur came out victorious against the Lodis and the Rajputs. The founder of the Mughal empire has received much acclaim from Pandit Jawaharlal Nehru for his fortitude in adversity, his daring against heavy odds, his swimming across many rivers, his love of flowers and fruits, and so on so forth. But his face, presented by himself in his *Tuzuk-i-Bāburī,* suffers irreparable damage if it is denuded of the rich hues of horrible cruelties in which he habitually indulged. The lurid details he provides of his repeated massacres of the infidels, leave no doubt that he was mighty proud of his performance. He was particularly fond of raising higher and higher towers of Hindu heads cut off during and after every battle he fought with them. He loved to sit in his royal tent to watch this spectacle. The prisoners were brought before him and butchered by his "brave" swordsmen. On one occasion, the ground flowed with so much blood and became so full of quivering carcases that his tent had to be moved thrice to a higher level. He lost no opportunity of capturing prisoners of war and amassing plunder. In the dynasty founded by him it was incumbent upon every king that he should style himself a *Ghāzī,* that is, slayer of infidels. When he broke vessels of wine on the eve of his battle with Rana Sangram Singh, he proclaimed that he would smash idols in a similar manner. And he destroyed temples wherever he saw them.

SHER SHAH SUR

Sher Shah Sur's name is associated in our textbooks with the Grand Trunk Road from Peshawar to Dacca, with caravanserais, and several other schemes of public welfare. It is true that he was not a habitual persecutor of Hindus before he became the emperor at Delhi. But he did not betray Islam when he became the supreme ruler. The test came at Raisen in 1543 AD. Shaykh Nurul Haq records in *Zubdat-ut-Tawārīkh* as follows: "In the year 950 H., Puranmal held occupation of the fort of Raisen.... He had 1000 women in his harem... and amongst them several Musulmanis whom he made to dance before him. Sher Khan with Musulman indignation resolved to conquer the fort. After he had been some time engaged in investing it, an accommodation was proposed and it was finally agreed that Puranmal with his family and children and 4000 Rajputs of note should be allowed to leave the fort unmolested. Several men learned in the law (of Islam) gave it as their opinion that they should all be slain, notwithstanding the solemn engagement which had been entered into. Consequently, the whole army, with the elephants, surrounded Puranmal's encampment. The Rajputs fought with desperate bravery and after killing their women and children and burning them, they rushed to battle and were annihilated to a man."

AKBAR

Humayun had hardly any time free from troubles to devote to the service of Islam. But his son, Akbar, made quite a good start as a *ghāzī*. He stabbed the half-dead Himu with his sword after the Second Battle of Panipat. The ritual was then followed by many more "brave warriors" of Islam led by Bairam Khan who drove their swords in the dead body. In 1568 AD Akbar ordered a general massacre at Chittor after the fort had fallen. Abul Fazl records in his *Akbar-Nāma* as follows. "There were 8,000 fighting Rajputs collected in the fortress, but there were more than 40,000 peasants who took part in watching and serving. From early dawn till midday the bodies of those ill-starred men were consumed by the majesty of the great warrior. Nearly 30,000 men were killed... When Sultan Alauddin (Khalji) took the fort after six months and seven days, the peasantry were not put to death as they had not engaged in fighting. But on this occasion they had shown great zeal and activity. Their excuses after the emergence of victory were of no avail, and orders were given for a general massacre." Akbar thus improved on the record of Alauddin Khalji. Watching the war and serving the warriors were re-interpreted as acts of war! To top it all, Akbar travelled post-haste to Ajmer where he offered profuse thanks to Allah and the Prophet, and his (Akbar's) patron saint, Muinuddin Chishti, and issued a *Fathnāma* in which many appropriate verses of the Quran were cited in order to prove that he had followed faithfully in the footsteps of the Prophet.

JAHANGIR

Jahangir was primarily a drunkard and a sadist scoundrel. He was too indolent to keep his promise, given to Nawab Murtaza

Khan at the time of his accession, that he would uphold the Shariat. He was too much devoted to women and the wine-cup to care much for Allah and the Prophet. But he encouraged conversions to Islam by giving daily allowances to the converts. In the very first year of his reign, he tortured Guru Arjun Dev to death. His contempt for Hindus comes out clearly in his *Tuzuk-i-Jahāngīrī*: "A Hindu named Arjun lived in Govindwal on the bank of river Beas in the garb of a saint and in ostentation. From all sides cowboys and idiots became his fast followers. The business had flourished for three or four generations. For a long time it had been in my mind to put a stop to this *dukān-e-bātil* (mart of falsehood) or to bring him into the fold of Islam." According to other accounts, he asked the Guru to include some *sūrahs* of the Quran in the *Ādi Grantha,* which the Guru refused to do. In the eighth year of his reign, he destroyed the temple of Bhagwat at Ajmer. He persecuted the Jains in Gujarat, and ordered that Jain monks should not be seen in his kingdom on pain of death. Finally, he sent Murtaza Khan to Kangra for reducing that city of temples. The siege lasted for 20 months at the end of which he himself went to Kangra for slaughtering cows in that sacred place of Hindus, and building a mosque where none had existed before.

SHAH JAHAN

The pendulum started swinging towards the true spirit of Islam at the very start of Shah Jahan's reign in 1628 AD. Its outer symbol was the reappearance of the beard on the face of the emperor. Abdul Hamid Lahori records in his *Bādshāhnāma*: "It had been brought to the notice of His Majesty that during the late reign many idol temples had been begun, but remained unfinished at Benares, the great stronghold of infidelism. The infidels were now desirous of completing them. His Majesty, the defender of the faith, gave orders that at Benares, and throughout all his dominions in every place, all temples that had been begun should be cast down. It was now reported from the province of Allahabad that 76 temples had been destroyed in the district of Benares." That was in 1633 AD.

In 1635 AD, Shah Jahan's soldiers captured some ladies of the royal Bundela family after Jujhar Singh and his sons failed to kill them in the time-honoured Rajput tradition. In the words of Jadunath Sarkar, "Mothers and daughters of kings, they were robbed of their religion and forced to lead the infamous life of the Mughal harem." Shah Jahan himself made a triumphal entry into Orchha, the capital of the Bundelas, demolished the lofty and massive temple of Bir Singh Dev, and raised a mosque in its place. Two sons and one grandson of Jujhar Singh who were of tender age, were made Musalmans. Another son of Jujhar Singh, Udaybhan, and a minister, Shyam Dawa, had fled to Golconda where they were captured by Qutbul-Mulk and sent to Shah Jahan. According to *Bādshāhnāma* again, "Udaybhan and Shyam Dawa, who were of full age, were offered the alternative of Islam or death. They chose the latter and were sent to hell."

AURANGZEB

With the coming of Aurangzeb, the policy of *sulah-i-kul* (peace with all) initiated by Akbar in the later part of his reign suffered a complete reversal. Aurangzeb had started his career as a *but-shikan* (iconoclast) 13 years before he ascended the throne at Delhi. According to *Mirāt-i-Ahmadī*, the temple of Chintaman situated close to Sarashpur (Gujarat) and built by Sitaldas jeweller was converted into a mosque named *Quwwat-ul-Islām* (might of Islam) by order of Prince Aurangzeb in 1645 AD. A cow was slaughtered to "solemnise" the "ceremony". Three years after he became king, he sent Mir Jumla on an expedition to Cooch Bihar. Mir Jumla demolished all temples in that city and erected mosques in their stead. The general himself wielded a battle-axe to break the image of Narayana.

In 1665 AD, it was reported to Aurangzeb that the temples he had demolished in Gujarat during his viceroyalty had been re-built by the Hindus. He immediately issued a *farmān* to the governor of Gujarat which said: "In Ahmedabad and other parganas of Gujarat in the days before my accession temples were destroyed by my order. They have been repaired and idol-worship resumed. Carry out the former order." In 1666 AD, he ordered the *faujdār* of Mathura to remove a stone railing which had been presented by Dara Shukoh to the temples of Keshav Rai. He explained: "In the Muslim faith it is a sin even to look at a temple and this Dara had restored a railing in a temple!"

A general policy towards Hindu temples was proclaimed in April 1669. *Maasir-i-Ālamgīrī* records: "On the 17th of Zil Kada 1079 (9th April 1669) it reached the ears of His Majesty, the protector of the faith, that in the provinces of Thatta, Multan, and Benares, but especially in the latter, foolish Brahmans were in the habit of expounding frivolous books in their schools, and that students and learners, Muslims as well as Hindus, went there, even from long distances, led by a desire to become acquainted with the wicked sciences they taught. The Director of the Faith, consequently, issued orders to all governors of provinces to destroy with a willing hand the schools and temples of the infidels and they were strictly enjoined to put an entire stop to the teaching and practising of idolatorous forms of worship. On the 15th Rabiul-akhir (end September) it was reported to his religious Majesty, leader of the unitarians, that in obedience to order, the government officers had destroyed the temple of Bishnath at Benares."

Maasir-i-Ālamgīrī continues: "In the month of Ramzan 980 H. (January 1670) this justice-loving monarch, the constant enemy of tyrants, commanded the destruction of the Hindu temple of Mathura known by the name of Dehra Keshav Rai, and soon that stronghold of falsehood was levelled with the ground. On the same spot was laid, with great expense, the foundation of a vast mosques... Glory be to Allah who has given us the faith of Islam that in this reign of the destroyer of false gods, an undertaking so difficult of attainment has been brought to a successful culmination. The richly jewelled idols taken from the infidel temples were transferred to Agra and there placed beneath the steps leading to the Nawab Begum Sahib's (Jahanara's) mosque in order that they might be pressed under foot by the true believers. Mathura changed its name into Islamabad and was thus called in all official documents."

In the same year, Sitaramji temple at Soron was destroyed as also the shrine of Devi Patan at Gonda. News came from Malwa also that the local governor had sent 400 troopers to destroy all temples around Ujjain. According to *Muraqāt-i-Abul Hasan*, civil officers, agents of *jāgirdārs*, *karoris* and *amlas* from Cuttack in Orissa to Medinipur in Bengal were instructed as follows: "Every idol house built during the last 10 or 12 years....should be demolished without delay. Also, do not allow the crushed Hindus and despicable infidels to repair their old temples. Reports of the destruction of temples should be sent to the court under the seal of the *qazis* and attested by pious Shaikhs."

In 1672 AD, several thousand Satnamis were slaughtered near Narnaul in Mewat for which act of "heroism" Radandaz Khan was titled Shuja'at Khan with the *mansab* of 3000 and 2000 horse. In 1675 AD, Guru Tegh Bahadur was tortured to death for his resistance against the forcible conversion of the Hindus of Kashmir. The destruction of *gurudwāras* thereafter is a well-known story which our secularists have succeeded in suppressing because the Akali brand Sikhs have been forging ties of friendship with Islam as against their parent faith, Hindu Dharma.

The year 1679 AD was the year of triumph for the "true faith". On April 2, *jizyah* was reimposed on Hindus to "spread Islam and put down the practice of infidelism". The Hindus of Delhi and around organised a protest and blocked Aurangzeb's way to the Jami Masjid on one Friday. The mighty Mughal Emperor ordered his elephants to be driven through the mass of men. Many were trampled to death. Shivaji also wrote a letter of protest from distant Maharashtra. But it fell on deaf ears. *Mirāt-i-Ahmadī* records: "Darab Khan was sent with a strong force to punish the Rajputs of Khandela and demolish the great temples of that place. He attacked the place on 8th March 1679 A.D. and pulled down the temples of Khandela and Sanula and all other temples in the neighbourhood." *Maasir-i-Ālamgīrī* adds: "On 25 May 1679 A.D. Khan Jahan Bahadur arrived from Jodhpur bringing with him several cart-loads of idols, taken from the Hindu temples that had been demolished. His Majesty gave him great praise. Most of these idols were adorned with precious stones. It was ordered that some of them should be cast away in the outer offices and the remainder placed beneath the steps of the grand mosque, there to be trampled under foot. There they lay a long time until at last not a vestige of them was left."

The year 1680 AD brought an equally "rich harvest" for Islam. *Maasir-i-Ālamgīrī* goes ahead: "On 6th January 1680 A.D. Prince Mohammad Azam and Khan Jahan Bahadur obtained permission to visit Udaipur. Ruhullah Khan and Yakkattāz Khan also proceeded thither to effect the destruction of the temples of the idolators. These edifices situated in the vicinity of the Rana's palace were among the wonders of the age, and had been erected by the infidels to the ruin of their souls and the loss of their wealth... Pioneers destroyed the images. On 24th January the king visited the tank of Udayasagar. His Majesty ordered all three of the Hindu temples to be levelled with the ground. On 29th January Hasan Ali Khan made his appearance... and stated that... 172 temples in the neighbouring districts had been destroyed. His Majesty proceeded to Chitor on 22nd February. Temples to the number of 63 were destroyed. Abu Tarab who had been commissioned to effect the destruction of idol temples of Amber, reported in person on 10th August that 66 temples had been levelled to the ground." The temple of Someshwar in western Mewar was also destroyed at a later date in the same year. It may be mentioned that unlike Jodhpur and Udaipur, Amber was the capital of a state loyal to the Mughal emperor.

According to *Kalimāt-i-Tayyibāt*, Aurangzeb wrote to Zulfiqar Khan and Mughal Khan that "the demolition of a temple is possible at any time, as it cannot walk away from it place". Even so, he was annoyed by the solid strength of temples in Maharashtra. *Kalimāt-i-Aurangzeb* reproduces his following message to Ruhullah Khan: "The houses of this country are exceedingly strong and built solely of the stone and iron. The hatchet-men of the government in course of my marching do not get sufficient manpower and time to destroy and raze the temples of infidels that meet the eye on the way. You should appoint a *darogha* who may afterwards destroy them at leisure and dig up their foundations." Aurangzeb himself acted as such a *darogha* in one instance. He reports in *Kalimāt-i-Aurangzeb:* "The village of Satara near Aurangabad was my hunting ground. Here on the top of hill stood a temple with an image of Khande Rai. By Allah's grace I demolished it and forbade the temple dancers to ply their shameful trade."

Demolition of Hindu temples remained Aurangzeb's pastime during his long campaign in the South. Khafi Khan records in his *Muntakhāb-ul-Lubāb*: "On the capture of Golconda, the Emperor appointed Abdur Rahim Khan as censor of the city of Haiderābād with orders to put down infidel practices and innovations, and destroy the temples and build mosques on the sites." That was in 1687 AD. In 1690 AD, he ordered destruction of temples at Ellora, Trimbakeshwar, Narasinghpur, and Pandharpur. In 1698 AD, the story was repeated at Bijapur. According to *Mirāt-i-Ahmadī*: "Hamid-ud-din Khan Bahadur who had been deputed to destroy the temples of Bijapur and build mosques there, returned to court after carrying out the order and was praised by the Emperor." As late as 1705 AD, two years before he died, "the emperor, summoning Muhammad Khalil and Khidmat Rai, the *darogha* of hatchet-men...ordered them to demolish the temple of Pandharpur, and to take the butchers of the camp there and slaughter cows in the temple." Cow-slaughter at a temple site was a safeguard against Hindus rebuilding it on the same spot.

The story can be continued to cover similar crimes committed by later Muslim monarchs and chieftains. But I am not continuing it because my theme at present is medieval India under Muslim rule, which period ended with the death of Aurangzeb.

The magnitude of crimes credited to Muslim monarchs by the medieval Muslim historians, was beyond measure. With a few exceptions, Muslim king and commanders were monsters who stopped at no crime when it came to their Hindu subjects. But what strikes as more significant is the broad pattern of those crimes. The pattern is that of a *jihād* in which the *ghāzīs* of Islam

1) invade infidel lands; 2) massacre as many infidel men, women, and children, particularly Brahmins, as they like *after* winning a victory; 3) capture the survivors to be sold as slaves; 4) plunder every place and person; 5) demolish idolatrous places of worship and build mosques in their places; and 6) defile idols which are flung into public squares or made into steps leading to mosques.

Still more significant is the fact that this is exactly the pattern 1) revealed by Allah in the Quran; 2) practised, perfected and pre-scribed by the Prophet in his own life-time; 3) followed by the pious Khalifas of Islam in the first 35 years of Islamic imperial-ism; 4) elaborated in the Hadis and hundreds of commentaries with meticulous attention to detail; 5) certified by the Ulama and the Sufis of Islam in all ages including our own; and 6) followed by all Muslim monarchs and chieftains who aspired for name and fame in this life, and houris and beardless boys hereafter.

It is, therefore, poor apologetics to blame the Islamized Turks alone of being barbarous. Islamic barbarism was shared in equal measure by all races and communities who were forced or lured into the fold of Islam — the Arabs, the Turks, the Persians, the Pathans, the Hindu converts. The conclusion in inescapable that Islam brutalizes all those who embrace it. And that is where the blame should be laid in all reason and justice.

We can now return to the NCERT guideline which proclaims that the conflict between Hindus and Muslims in medieval India shall be regarded as political rather than religious. There is no justification for such a characterisation of the conflict. The Mus-lims at least were convinced that they were waging a religious war against the Hindu infidels. The conflict can be regarded as political only if the NCERT accepts the very valid proposition that Islam has never been a religion, and that it started and has remained a political ideology of terrorism with unmistakable to-talitarian trends and imperialist ambitions. The first premises as well as the procedures of Islam bear a very close resemblance to those of Communism and Nazism. Allah is only the predecessor of the Forces of Production invoked by the Communists, and of the Aryan Race invoked by the Nazis.

CHAPTER VIII

THE MYTH OF MUSLIM EMPIRE IN INDIA

The apologists of Islam and their secularist lick-spittles argue that if the Muslim conquerors had practised such systematic, extensive, and continued terror against Hindus and Hinduism as has been recorded by the Muslim historians of medieval India, Hindus could not have survived as an overwhelming majority at the end of the long spell of Muslim rule.

The logic here is purely deductive (formal). Suppose a person is subjected to a murderous assault, but he survives because he fights back. Deductively it can be concluded that the person never suffered a murderous assault because otherwise he could not have been alive! But this conclusion has little relevance to the facts of the case.

My sixth question, therefore, is: Did Hindus survive as a majority in their own homeland because the Islamic invaders did not employ sufficient force to kill or convert them, or because, though defeated again and again by the superior military skill of the invaders, Hindu princes did not give up resistance and came back again and again to reconquer their lost kingdoms, to fight yet another battle, yet another day, till the barbarians were brought to book?

Before I answer this question, I should like to warn against a very widely prevalent though a very perverse version of Indian history. In this popular version, Indian history has been reduced to a history of foreign invaders who were able to enter India from time to time — the so-called Aryans, the Iranians, the Greeks, the Parthians, the Scythians, the Kushanas, the Hunas, the Arabs, the Turks, the Pathans, the Mughals, the Persians, the Portuguese, the Dutch, the French, and the British. The one impression which this version of Indian history leaves, is that India has always been a no-man's land which any armed bandit could come and occupy at any time, and that Hindus have always been a "meek mob" which has always bowed before every "superior" race.

Muslims in India and elsewhere have been led to believe by

the mullahs and Muslim historians that the conquest of India by Islam started with the invasion of Sindh by Muhammad bin Qasim in 712 AD, was resumed by Mahmud Ghaznavi in 1000 AD, and completed by Muhammad Ghuri when he defeated the Chauhans of Ajmer and the Gahadvads of Kanauj in the last decade of the 12th century. Muslims of India in particular have been persuaded to look back with pride on those six centuries, if not more, when India was ruled by Muslim emperors. In this make-belief, the British rulers are treated as temporary intruders who *cheated* Islam of its Indian empire for a hundred years. So also the "Hindu Banias", who succeeded the British in 1947 AD. Muslims are harangued every day, in every mosque and *madrasah,* not to rest till they reconquer the rest of India which, they are told, rightfully belongs to Islam.

The academic historians also agree that India was ruled by Muslim monarchs from the last decade of the 12th century to the end of the 18th. The standard textbooks of history, therefore, narrate medieval Indian history in terms of a number of Muslim imperial dynasties ruling from Delhi — the Mamluks (Slaves), the Khaljis, the Tughlaqs, the Sayyids, the Lodis, the Surs, the Mughals. The provincial Muslim dynasties with their seats at Srinagar, Lahore, Multan, Thatta, Ahmedabad, Mandu, Burhan-pur, Daulatabad, Gulbarga, Bidar, Golconda, Bijapur, Madurai, Gaur, Jaunpur, and Lucknow fill the gaps during periods of imperial decline.

It is natural that in this version of medieval Indian history the recurring Hindu resistance to Islamic invaders, imperial as well as provincial, looks like a series of sporadic revolts occasioned by some minor grievances of purely local character, or led by some petty upstarts for purely personal gain. The repeated Rajput resurgence in Rajasthan, Bundelkhand and the Ganga-Yamuna Doab; the renewed assertion of independence by Hindu princes at Devagiri, Warrangal, Dvarasamudra and Madurai; the rise of the Vijayanagara Empire; the farflung fight offered by the Marathas; and the mighty movement of the Sikhs in the Punjab — all these then get readily fitted into the framework of a far-flung and enduring Muslim empire. And the Hindu heroes who led this resistance for several centuries get reduced to ridiculous rebels who disturbed public peace at intervals but who were always put down.

But this version of medieval Indian history is, at its best, only an interpretation based on preconceived premises and propped up by a highly selective summarisation, or even invention, of facts. There is ample room for another interpretation based on more adequate premises, and borne out by a far better systematisation of known facts.

What are the facts? Do they bear out the interpretation that India was fully and finally conquered by Islam, and that the Muslim empire in India was a finished fabric before the British stole it for themselves by fraudulent means?

MUSLIM INVASIONS WERE NO WALK-OVER

The so-called conquest of Sindh first.

Having tried a naval invasion of India through Thana, Broach, and Debal from 634 to 637 AD, the Arabs tried the land route on the north-west during AD 650-711. But the Khyber Pass was blocked by the Hindu princes of Kabul and Zabul who inflicted many defeats on the Arabs, and forced them to sign treaties of non-aggression. The Bolan pass was blocked by the Jats of Kikan. Al Biladuri writes in his *Futūh-ul-Buldān*: "At the end of 38 H. or the beginning of 39 H. (659 A.D.) in the Khilafat of Ali...Harras...went with the sanction of the Khalif to the same frontier... He and those who were with him, saving a few, were slain in the land of Kikan in the year 42 H. (662 A.D.). In the year 44 H. (664 A.D) and in the days of Khalif Muawiya, Muhallab made war on the same frontier...The enemy opposed him and killed him and his followers...Muawiya sent Abdullah...to the frontier of Hind. He fought in Kikan and captured booty... He stayed near the Khalif some time and then returned to Kikan, when the Turks (Hindus) called their forces together and slew him."

Next, the Arabs tried the third land route, via Makran. Al Biladuri continues: "In the reign of the same Muawiya, Chief Ziyad appointed Sinan... He proceeded to the frontier and hav-

ing subdued Makran and its cities by force, he stayed there...
Ziyad then appointed Rashid... He proceeded to Makran but he
was slain fighting against the Meds (Hindus)... Abbad, son of
Ziyad then made war on the frontier of Hind by way of Seistan.
He fought the inhabitants... but many Musulmans perished...
Ziyad next appointed Al Manzar. Sinan had taken it but its inhabitants had been guilty of defection... He (Al Manzar) died
there... When Hajjaj...was governor of Iraq, Said...was appointed to Makran and its frontiers. He was opposed and slain
there. Hajjaj then appointed Mujja...to the frontier... Mujja died
in Makran after being there a year...Then Hajjaj sent Ubaidullah
...against Debal. Ubaidullah being killed, Hajjaj wrote to Budail
...directing him to proceed to Debal... the enemy surrounded and
killed him. Afterwards, Hajjaj during the Khilafat of Walid,
appointed Mohammad, son of Qasim...to command on the
Sindhian frontier." That was in 712 AD.

Now compare this Arab record on the frontiers of India with
their record elsewhere. Within eight years of the Prophet's death,
they had conquered Persia, Syria, and Egypt. By 650 AD, they
had advanced upto the Oxus and the Hindu Kush. Between 640
and 709 AD they had reduced the whole of North Africa. They
had conquered Spain in 711 AD. But it took them 70 long years
to secure their first foothold on the soil of India. No historian
worth his salt should have the cheek to say that the Hindus have
always been an easy game for invaders.

Muhammad bin Qasim succeeded in occupying some cities
of Sindh. His successors led some raids towards the Punjab,
Rajasthan, and Saurashtra. But they were soon defeated, and
driven back. The Arab historians admit that "a place of refuge to
which the Muslims might flee was not to be found". By the
middle of the 8th century they controlled only the highly garri-
soned cities of Multan and Mansurah. Their plight in Multan is
described by Al Kazwin in *Asr-ul-Bilād* in the following words:
"The infidels have a large temple there, and a great idol...The
houses of the servants and devotees are around the temple, and
there are no idol worshippers in Multan besides those who dwell
in those precincts... *The ruler of Multan does not abolish this*

idol because he takes the large offerings which are brought to it... When the Indians make an attack upon the town, the Muslims bring out the idol, and when the infidels see it about to be broken or burnt, they retire." (emphasis added). So much for Islamic monotheism of the Arabs and their military might. They, the world-conquerors, failed to accomplish anything in India except a short-lived raid.

It was some two hundred years later, in 963 AD, that Alptigin the Turk was successful in seizing Ghazni, the capital of Zabul. It was his successor Subuktigin who seized Kabul from the Hindu Shahiyas shortly before he died in 997 AD. His son, Mahmud Ghaznavi, led many expeditions into India between 1000 and 1027 AD. The details of his destructive frenzy are too well-known to be repeated. What concerns us here is the facile supposition made by historians in general that Mahmud was not so much interested in establishing an empire in India as in demolishing temples, plundering treasures, capturing slaves, and killing the *kāfirs*. This supposition does not square with his seizure of the Punjab west of the Ravi, and the whole of Sindh. The conclusion is unavoidable that though Mahmud went far into the heartland of Hindustan and won many victories, he had to beat a hasty retreat every time in the face of Hindu counterattacks. This point is proved by the peril in which he was placed by the Jats of the Punjab during his return from Somnath in 1026 AD.

The same Jats and the Gakkhars gave no end of trouble to the Muslim occupants of Sindh and the Punjab after Mahmud was dead. Another 150 years were to pass before another Islamic invader planned a conquest of India. This was Muhammad Ghuri. His first attempt towards Gujarat in 1178 AD met with disaster at the hands of the Chaulukyas, and he barely escaped with his life. And he was carried half-dead from the battlefield of Tarain in 1191 AD. It was only in 1192 AD that he won his first victory against Hindus by resorting to a mean stratagem which the chivalrous Rajputs failed to see through.

THE TURKISH EMPIRE WAS TEMPORARY
Muhammad Ghuri conquered the Punjab, Sindh, Delhi, and

the Doab upto Kanauj. His general Qutbuddin Aibak extended the conquest to Ajmer and Ranthambhor in Rajasthan, Gwalior, Kalinjar, Mahoba and Khajuraho in Bundelkhand, and Katehar and Badaun beyond the Ganges. His raid into Gujarat was a failure in the final round though he succeeded in sacking and plundering Anahilwar Patan. Meanwhile, Bakhtyar Khalji had conquered Bihar and Bengal north and west of the Hooghly. He suffered a disastrous defeat when he tried to advance into Assam.

But by the time Muhammad Ghuri was assassinated by the Gakkhars in 1206 AD, and Aibak assumed power over the former's domain in India, Kalinjar had been reconquered by the Chandellas, Ranthambhor had renounced vassalage to Delhi, Gwalior had been reoccupied by the Pratihars, the Doab was up in arms under the Gahadvad prince Harishchandra, and the Katehar Rajputs had reasserted their independence beyond the Ganges. The Yadavbhatti Rajputs around Alwar had cut off the imperial road to Ajmer. Aibak was not able to reconquer any of these areas before he died in 1210 AD.

Aibak's successor, Iltutmish, succeeded in retaking Ranthambhor and Gwalior, and in widening his base around Ajmer. But he suffered several defeats at the hands of the Guhilots of Nagda, the Chauhans of Bundi, the Paramars of Malwa, and the Chandellas of Bundelkhand. Beyond the Ganges, the Katehar Rajputs had consolidated their hold which the Sultan could not shake. The Doab was still offering a very stiff resistance. His grip on Ajmer had also started slipping by the time he died in 1236 AD.

The Sultanate suffered a steep decline during the reigns of Razia, Bahram, Masud, and Mahmud of the Shamsi dynasty founded by Iltutmish, though its dissolution was prevented by Balban who wielded effective power from 1246 AD onwards. The Muslim position in Bengal was seriously threatened by Hindu Orissa. Another Muslim invasion of Assam ended in yet another disaster in which the Muslim general lost his life and a whole Muslim army was annihilated. Hindu chieftains now started battering the Muslim garrison towns in Bihar. Near Delhi, the Chandellas advanced up to Mathura. The Rajputs from Alwar made raids as far as Hansi, and became a terror for Muslims even in the environs of Delhi. Balban's successes against this rising tide of Hindu recovery were marginal. He suffered several set-backs. The Sultanate was once more reduced to a rump around Delhi when Balban died in 1289 AD.

Dr. R.C. Majumdar has summed up the situation so far in the following words: "India south of the Vindhyas was under Hindu rule in the 13th century. Even in North India during the same century, there were powerful kingdoms not yet subjected to Muslim rule, or still fighting for their independence... Even in that part of India which acknowledged the Muslim rule, there was continual defiance and heroic resistance by large or small bands of Hindus in many quarters, so that successive Muslim rulers had to send well-equipped military expeditions, again and again, against the same region... As a matter of fact, the Muslim authority in Northern India, throughout the 13th century, was tantamount to a miltary occupation of a large number of impor-tant centres without any effective occupation, far less a system-atic administration of the country at large."

Jalaluddin Khalji failed to reconquer any land which had been lost by Muslims during the earlier reign. Alauddin was far more successful. His generals, Ulugh Khan and Nusrat Khan, were able to conquer Gujarat in 1298 AD. But they were beaten back from Rathambhor which Alauddin could reduce only in 1301 AD. His conquest of Chittor in 1303 AD was shortlived as the Sisodias retook it soon after his death in 1316 AD. So was his conquest of Jalor in Rajasthan. His own as well Malik Kafur's expeditions against Devagiri in Maharashtra, Warrangal in Andhra Pradesh, Dvarsamudra in Karnataka, and Madurai in Tamil Nadu, were nothing more than raids because Hindu princes reasserted their independence in all these capitals soon after the invaders left. And the Khalji empire collapsed as soon as Alauddin died in 1316 AD. Ghiyasuddin Tughlaq had to inter-vene in 1320 AD to save the remnants from being taken over by Hindus from Gujarat who had been nominally converted to Islam.

Ghiyasuddin Tughlaq was succesful in conquering south

and east Bengal. But he could not completely subdue Tirhut in Bihar. His son Jauna Khan suffered defeat in 1321 AD when he tried to reconquer Warrangal, and had to mount another attack in 1323 AD before he could reduce it. But by 1326 AD Prataparudra was back in power. In 1324 AD Jauna Khan had been beaten back from the borders of Orissa. He was more successful when he came to power as Muhammad Tughlaq. He consolidated his hold over Devagiri, conquered the small kingdom of Kampili on the Tungbhadra, and forced Dvarasamudra to pay tribute to the imperial authority of Delhi. Madurai also came to be included in his empire. He transferred his capital to Devagiri in order to keep a close watch on Hindu resurrection in the South, and for establishing another centre of Islamic power in India. But at the very start of his reign he had been defeated by Maharana Hammir of Mewar, taken prisoner, and released only after he ceded all claims to Ajmer, Ranthambhor and Nagaur, besides payment of 50 lakhs of rupees as indemnity. And his empire south of the Vindhyas was lost to Delhi in his own life-time, and Delhi's hold over large areas even in the North disappeared soon after his death in 1351 AD.

Firuz Shah Tughlaq was able to keep together the rump for some time. His expedition to Orissa was nothing more than a successful raid. And he had to lead annual expeditions against the Katehar Rajputs north of the Ganges. His successors could not keep even the rump in the north. It broke down completely after Timur's invasion in 1399 AD. Meanwhile, the great Vijayanagara Empire had consolidated Hindu power south of the Krishna. Rajasthan was ruled by defiant Rajput princes led by Mewar. Orissa had fully recovered from the devastation of Firuz Shah Tughlaq's raid.

The Sayyids who succeeded the Tughlaqs were hardly an imperial dynasty when they started in 1414 AD. Their hold did not extend beyond Etawah (U.P.) in the east, and Mewat (Haryana) in the south. Khizr Khan tried to restore the empire in the north but without success. Mubarak Shah was able to recover the Punjab and Multan before the Sayyids were supplanted by the Lodis in 1451 AD.

Bahlol Lodi reduced the Muslim principality of Jaunpur in 1457 AD. But Sikandar Lodi failed to subdue Gwalior, Rajasthan, and Baghelkhand. He removed his capital to Agra in order to plan a conquest of Malwa and Rajasthan. But it bore no fruit. The Lodi "empire" more or less broke down under Ibrahim Lodi. By this time, Mewar under Rana Sanga had emerged as the strongest state in North India. Orissa stood its ground against Muslim Bengal to its north and the Bahmanis to its south. The power of Vijayanagara attained its acme under Krishnadevaraya (1505-1530 AD).

The situation during the 14th and the 15th centuries has been summed up by Dr. R.C. Majumdar in the following words: "The Khalji empire rose and fell during the brief period of twenty years (A.D 1300-1320). The empire of Muhammed bin Tughlaq... broke up within a decade of his accession (A.D. 1325), and before another decade was over, the Turkish empire passed away for ever.... Thus barring two every short-lived empires under the Khaljis and Muhammad bin Tughlaq...there was no Turkish empire in India. This state of things continued for nearly two centuries and a half till the Mughals established a stable and durable empire in the second half of the sixteenth century A.D."

MUGHAL EMPIRE: A JOINT VENTURE

Babur won some renowned victories but hardly established an empire. Humayun lost to Sher Shah Sur, and failed to win back most of what Babur had won. Sher Shah added Ranthambhor and Ajmer to his empire in north India. But the fierce fight he faced in Marwar made him confess that he had almost lost an empire for a handful of millet. His rule lasted only for a brief span of five years (1540-1545 AD). The Sur "empire" became a shambles soon after, so much so that the Hindu general Himu was able to crown himself as Hemachandra Vikramaditya at Delhi in 1556 AD.

The Mughal empire founded by Akbar in 1556 AD proved more stable, and endured for 150 years. It also expanded in all directions till by the end of the 17th century it covered almost the whole of India except the extreme south. But the credit for

Mughal success must go largely to Akbar's recognition of power realities, and reconciliation with the Rajputs by suspension of several tenets of a typically Islamic state. It was the Rajput generals and soldiers who won many of the victories for which the Mughals took credit. The Rajput states in Rajasthan and Bundelkhand were vassals of the Mughal emperor only in name. For all practical purposes, they were allies of the Mughals who had to keep them in good humour. And Mewar kept aloft the flag of Hindu defiance throughout the period of effective Mughal rule.

The Mughal empire started breaking up very fast when Aurangzeb reversed Akbar's policy of accommodating the Hindus, and tried to re-establish a truly Islamic state based on terror, and oppression of the "non-believers". Rajasthan and Bundelkhand reasserted their independence during his life-time. So did the Jats around Bharatpur and Mathura. The Marathas dug Aurangzeb's grave when they made imperial seats such as Ahmadnagar and Aurangabad unsafe in spite of large Mughal garrisons, and invaded imperial territory as far as Khandesh and Gujarat. This Hindu resurgence shattered the Mughal empire within two decades of Aurangzeb's death in 1707 AD.

THE PROVINCIAL MUSLIM PRINCIPALITIES

Amongst the provincial Muslim principalities established by rebels and adventurers after the break-up of the Tughlaq empire, those of Bengal, Malwa, Gujarat, and the Bahmanis were notable. Hindu Orissa battled against Bengal till both of them were taken over by the Mughals. The Sisodias of Mewar engaged Gujarat and Malwa, and almost overcame them in the reign of Rana Sanga. Gujarat recovered for a short time only to be taken over by the Mughals. The Vijayanagara Empire contained the Bahmanis from southward expansion in a fierce struggle spread over more than two centuries, in which fortunes on both sides waxed and waned. The destruction of the metropolis at Vijayanagara did not lead to the destruction of the Vijayanagara Empire. It barred the path of Bijapur for another seventy years. Meanwhile, the Marathas had come to control large parts of

South India as nominal vassals of Ahmadnagar and Bijapur even before Shivaji appeared on the scene. And they were soon to deliver death blows to the remnants of the Bahmani empire which the Mughals hastened to incorporate in their own empire.

THE PROPER PERSPECTIVE

Reviewed as a whole, the period between the last decade of the 12th century and the first quarter of the 18th — the period which is supposed to be the period of Muslim empire in India — is nothing more than a period of long-drawn-out war between Hindu freedom fighters and the Muslim invaders. The Hindus lost many battles, and retreated again and again. But they recovered every time, and resumed the struggle so that eventually the enemy was worn out, defeated, and dispersed in the final round which started with the rise of Shivaji.

As we read the history of medieval India we find that only a few Hindu princes made an abject surrender before the proved superiority of Muslim arms. Muslim historians cite innumerable instances of how Hindus burnt or killed their womenfolk, and then died fighting to the last man. There were many instances of Muslims being defeated decisively by Hindu heroism. Many of the so-called Muslim conquests were mere raids which succeeded initially but the impact of which did not last for long. The account which Assam, Rajasthan, Bundelkhand, Orissa, Telingana, Tamil Nadu, Karnataka, Maharashtra, and the Punjab gave of themselves in successive waves of resistance and recovery, has not many parallels in human history.

It is, therefore, a travesty of truth to say that Islam enjoyed an empire in India for six centuries. What happened really was that Islam struggled for six centuries to conquer India for good, but failed in the final round in the face of stiff and continued Hindu resistance. Hali was not at all wrong when he mourned that the invincible armada of Hijaz which had swept over so many seas and rivers met its watery grave in the Ganges. Iqbal also wrote his *Shikwah* in sorrowful remembrance of the same failure. In fact, there is no dearth of Muslim poets and politicians who weep over the defeat of Islam in India in the past, and who look forward to a reconquest of India in the future. Hindus have survived as a majority in their motherland not because Islam spared any effort to conquer and convert them but because Islamic brutality met more than its equal in Hindu tenacity for freedom.

Nor is it anywhere near the truth to say that the British empire in India replaced an earlier Muslim empire. The effective political power in India had already passed into the hands of the Marathas, the Jats, and the Sikhs when the British started playing their imperialist game. The Muslim principalities in Bengal, Avadh, South India, Sindh, and the Punjab were no match for the Hindu might that had resurged. The Mughal emperor at Delhi by that time presented a pitiful picture of utter helplessness. The custodians of Islam in India were repeatedly inviting Ahmad Shah Abdali from across the border to come and rescue Islam from the abyss into which it had fallen.

CHAPTER IX

THE DETERMINANTS OF HINDU DEFEATS

It is true that Hindus resisted Islamic imperialism for a long time, and overcame it in the long run. But it would be foolish to forget that their failure for a long time in the face of an enemy with whom they had become familiar pretty soon, was of frightening proportions. It is this failure of the Hindus and not the defeat of the Muslim marauders which invites a serious review and reflection. I will, therefore, do my own loud thinking on this subject. For I feel very strongly that the lessons we may learn from these failures are still valid for us.

It is held by almost all historians of this period, including those who neither swear by Marxism nor apologise for Islam, that the Hindu failure had its source in the Hindu social system, particularly the caste structure. But that proposition does not stand a deeper probe. Moreover, the proposition is preposterous because it reverses the chronological sequence. The Hindu social system became moribund and the caste system rigid only *after* Hindus had lost political power. There is sufficient evidence to prove that on the eve of Islamic invasions, the Hindu social system did not harbour the defects which it developed at a later stage. It is my considered opinion that it was their highly organic social system which saved the Hindus from extinction in the initial stages, and provided the powerful impetus which propelled them to victory in the long run. Iran, Iraq, Syria, Egypt, and North Africa were engulfed by Islam because they did not have a social structure which could withstand the storm.

At a first glance, the Hindu failure looks like the failure of their art of warfare, pure and simple. The traditional Hindu warriors, particularly the Rajputs, were in no way inferior, if not superior, to the Turks in terms of valour and tenacity. Nor were the Muslim mercenaries any match for the Hindu warriors when it came to dedication to ideals of freedom and sense of honour and sacrifice. But the superiority of the Turkish art of warfare in terms of strategy, tactics, mobility, military morale, and arsenal set at nought the Hindu superiority and Muslim inferiority in many other respects.

At a second remove, the Hindu failure can be perceived as a political failure, a failure of their state system. In the initial stages at least, the larger Hindu states like the Shahiyas, the Chauhans, the Chandellas, the Gahadvads, and the Chaulukyas were far superior to the Islamic invaders in terms of financial means as well as manpower. But Hindus failed to mobilise these resources in any worthwhile manner. They could not have mobilised these resources even if they had wanted to, without radically reforming their state system. The decentralised and democratic character of the Hindu state, and the paucity of central revenue under the Hindu system of public finance, prevented Hindu princes from maintaining standing armies on a permanent war-footing. Hindu princes had to depend largely on levies recruited on the spur of the moment. And most of the time, these levies behaved no better than mobs. The larger the mob, the lower was its power to withstand assaults from solid phalanxes such as the Muslim conquerors brought to the battlefield. The battle could last only so long as the small number of trained and traditional Hindu warriors could sustain the shock. The Muslim war-machine on the other hand had been reared by a militarised state system, and was geared to withstand a stiffer strain.

But the deeper reason fails to be satisfied even by these explanations of the Hindu failure. Why did not the Hindus mend their art of warfare after they had seen the superiority of Muslim military methods? Why did the Hindus refuse to streamline their state system till it was too late? The military as well as political failure could have been overcome speedily if some deeper failure had not continued to linger for a long time. It is this deeper failure which I want to discuss in this chapter.

THE FOREMOST FAILURE: SPIRITUAL

To start with, what strikes me most is the steep decline in the Hindu spiritual perception. The sacred and philosophical literature produced by Hindus from the 5th century onwards compares very unfavourably with similar literature of an earlier age — the Mahabharata, the Ramayana, the earlier Puranas, the

Manusmriti. The earlier literature dwells naturally and effort-lessly on the Himalayan heights of the human soul, but at the same time it pays due attention to every detail of terrestrial life. The family, the clan, the village, the *janapada*, the *rāshṭra* — life at each of these levels is sustained by a *dharma* appropriate to the level and complexity of relationships involved. The *janmabhūmi*, the motherland, is equated with the *janani*, the lov-ing mother, and endowed with sanctity higher than that of heaven. Human society in its smaller and as well larger segments is an enabling environment in which the individual seeks *abhyudaya*, munadane welfare, as well as *nisśreyas,* spiritual salvation. Society has a lot to give to the individual in terms of upbringing, education, status within the brotherhood of the *varṇa*, and livelihood in the fraternity of the *jāti*. But society also demands a lot in terms of self-discipline, performance of duties due from one's station in life, and sacrifice which mostly means living for others. The *rājā,* the state, is an embodiment of the protecting power of the Divine, and demands in turn taxes and obedience to legitimate laws.

In the eyes of this highly vigilant spirituality, evil is as much present in human nature as the good, and manifests itself in as many ways as the good. This spirituality is, therefore, wide awake to every eruption of evil, individual as well as collective. It can spot evil at the ideological and the psychological level as easily as at the level of its physical manifestation or concrete action. And it recommends a combat with evil, *devāsura-saṁgrāma*, in every sphere of life. In this spirituality, there is no place for suffering evil silently, or for explaining it away, or for facing it with a subjective sanctimoniousness, howsoever el-evated the language that sanctimoniousness may employ. When Alexander had asked a Brahmin as to what they taught which inspired Hindu warriors to such high heroism, the Brahmin had replied in one sentence — "We teach our people to live with honour."

But the spiritual literature and philosophies of several centu-ries preceding and following the Islamic invasions, breathe an altogether different atmosphere. While it does not lose any of its

heights, its grip on life as lived in this world gets greatly loos-
ened. There is an insistent and increasing rejection of terrestrial
life, and turning one's back upon it is termed as the highest
human endeavour. Dharma is no more a comprehesive concept
embracing the wide wealth of human relationships; it is nar-
rowed down to specialised disciplines enjoined by the goal of
individual salvation. In fact, human relationships start getting
redefined as so many snares which entangle and encumber the
individual soul in its journey towards the supreme attainment.
Honour and heroism now become lower values when compared
to the herculean effort of breaking the shackles of *karma* and
getting across the ocean of rebirth. Most spiritual seekers now
not only take to *sannyāsa* but also go into seclusion in search of
samādhi, the mystic trance. *Tantra, mantra, maṇḍala* and *yantra*
follow in sequence till spirituality in most cases gets reduced to
some sort of an esoteric ritualism which is loath to subject itself
to any objective test of character or performance. Those who do
not feel drawn towards this highly elaborate but entirely subjective spirituality are now free to pursue *artha*, acquisitions, or
kāma, pleasures, or both, without any guidance from *dharma*.

Many students of the spiritual literature of this period have
hailed the medieval *siddhas* and the saints as harbingers of a
casteless society. They do not see the perspective in which *varṇa*
and *jāti* become irrelevant for the spiritual seekers of this period.
*The perspective is one of social indifference, not one of social
concern.* The *siddhas* and the saints are indifferent not only to
varṇa and *jāti*, but also to the *rājā* and the *rāshtra*. None of them
tells the princes that the supreme test of their prowess and
honour is the protection of their *prajā*. Some of them do bemoan
the terror, destruction, descreation, and spoliation perpetrated by
the Islamic invaders. But the complaint is addressed to God
Almighty who allows such horrible things to happen. The voice
which a Valmiki or a Vyasa would have raised for resistance to
and destruction of the *dasyu*, marauder, and the *ātatāyī*, gangster,
is missing. Samartha Ramdasa is the only exception.

It is small wonder, therefore, that Hindu saints of this period
failed to see Islam with the eyes of a wholesome spirituality

practised in earlier ages. They took at face value the professions of Islam that it was a religion like one of their own. Some of them were impressed by Islamic monotheism, and started denouncing the multiplicity of their own Gods and Goddesses. None of them could see that the *Kalimah* — there is no god but Allah and Muhammad is his last prophet — could emanate only from a beastly rather than a religions consciousness. Not a single Hindu saint made the effort to see or succeeded in seeing through the professions of Islam or the piety of its sufis, and exposing the sin and the sham masquerading as religion and sainthood. The *Nirguna* saints did question the exclusive claims of Islam. But none of them questioned its claim as an alternate path of salvation. And all of them assailed Brahmanism and polytheism.

The thinkers and philosophers of this period proved worse than the saints in this respect. They argued back and forth on all possible positions in metaphysics, ethics, aesthetics, logic, linguistics, social ceremonies, and religious rituals. But none of them made a systematic or serious study of Islam, or traced to its scriptural source its terrorism and cruelty. The saints at least soothed and strengthened their people by their songs and sermons. The thinkers and philosophers cannot claim even that much credit. They only divided their people by their highly sectarian scholasticism. A majority of the Muslims were Hindu converts who had been forced or lured into the fold of Islam which sat lightly on them for a long time. Hindu society closed its doors on them, and condemned them to permanent and progressive alienation. The results would have been radically different if Hindu thinkers and philosophers had rejected Islam, and won back the converts to Islam into their mother society.

THE SECOND FAILURE: CULTURAL

The failure of Hindu spiritual perception had something, perhaps much, to do with the failure of the Hindu cultural vision. There was a lapse of historical memory and cultural tradition about the essential unity, integrity, and sanctity of what the Mahabharata, the Ramayana, the Puranas, and the Dharmashastras had clearly defined as Bharatavarsha. This vast

land which Islam has dismembered in due course into the separate states of Afghanistan, Pakistan, Hindustan, and Bangladesh
had been a single indivisible whole since times immemorial.
Bharatavarsha had been termed by the ancients as the cradle of
varṇāśrama-dharma, witness to the wheel of the *caturyugas,* and
the *kshetra* for *chākravārtya,* spiritual as well as political. This
historical memory and cultural tradition was alive as late as the
imperial Guptas. Kalidasa had clothed it in immortal poetry in
his far-famed *Raghuvaṁśa.*

This failure of Hindu cultural vision had serious consequences. Hindus failed to organise a collective effort to guard the
frontiers of Bharatavarsha. Hindu princes in the interior did not
rally round Raja Dahir when Muhammad bin Qasim violated the
sacred soil of Sindh. They made some better effort when the
Hindu Shahiyas of Udbhandapur were challenged by Subuktigin.
But the effort fizzled out before long, because very few of them
had their heart in it. Hindu princes by now had taken a deep dose
of Kautalya's *Arthaśāstra* which, along with Vatsyayana's
Kāmasūtra, had become a prime part of their political education.
In this sterile statecraft, centred on the politics of the
maṇḍalayoni, one's neighbour was always an enemy, and the
enemy of an enemy always a friend! Hindu princes, therefore,
failed to hang together in the face of a common calamity. In the
event, they were hanged separately.

THE THIRD FAILURE: MENTAL

The third failure which was closely linked with the first two
was the failure of mental alertness to what was happening in the
world around. Hindu merchants were still selling the products of
Indian agriculture and industry in all lands invaded by Islam.
Hindu saints, particularly the Buddhist monks, were still practising their austerities and preaching their sermons in their far-
flung monasteries in Iran and Khorasan. But none of them could
see the storm that was rising on the sands of Arabia and sowing
a harvest of mass slaughter, pillage, plunder and enslavement,
not even when it swept over neighbouring lands. They waited
where they were till they were slaughtered and/or plundered in

their own turn, or, if they fled back home, they did not say the word that could have served as a warning. Nor were the Hindu princes in a mental mood to heed any warning even if it had been tendered to them. An awareness of what was happening in neighbouring lands was no more needed by them. Each one of them was busy with his immediate neighbours. There was no lack of martial spirit, or sense of honour, or sentiments of chivalry in them. But all this wealth of character was wasted in proving their prowess over primacy of the right to a first dip in holy rivers and tanks, or to the hands of pretty princesses. What they lacked was statesmanship which is always an outcome of an alert and wide-ranging mind. They learnt neither from their own defeats, nor from the victories of the enemy. They mended neither their statecraft, nor their system of revenue, nor their military establishment, nor yet their art of warfare.

It cannot be maintained that Islam did not provide an ample opportunity to Hindu saints, philosophers and princes to understand its true character and role. Before the armies of Islam invaded India, the sufis had settled down in many parts of India, built mosque and khanqahs and started their work of conversion. They were the sappers and miners of Islamic invasions which followed in due course. Muinuddin Chishti was not the first "saint" of Islam to send out an invitation to an Islamic invader to come and kill the *kāfirs*, desecrate their shrines, and plunder their wealth. He was following in the footsteps of earlier Islamic "saints" functioning as fifth-columnists for Muhammad bin Qasim and Mahmud Ghaznavi. There was an interval of two and a half centuries between the Arab demonstration in Sindh of what Islam had in store for the Hindus, and the horrors let loose by Mahmud Ghaznavi. Again, there was another interval of a century and a half between the invasions of Mahmud Ghaznavi and those of Muhammad Ghuri. But neither the Hindu saints, nor the Hindu philosophers, nor the Hindu princes could see the sufis for what they were in essence, or draw any worthwhile conclusions about the character of Islam.

This triple Hindu failure on the spiritual, cultural, and mental levels prevented Hindu society from evolving and pursuing policies which were imperative in the unprecedented situation, and which would have saved it from the permanent scourge of a malignant fraternity embedded in its very heart.

THE POLICIES WHICH WERE NOT PURSUED

The first need of the situation was a centre round which Hindus could rally, and from which Hindu resistance to the Islamic invasion could be directed. The effectiveness of such a centre was demonstrated first in the South under Vijayanagara, secondly in Mewar under Maharana Sanga, thirdly in Maharashtra under Shivaji, and lastly in the Punjab under Banda Bahadur. But these centres crytallised too late. A nationwide centre established earlier could have contained Islamic imperialism at the borders of Bharatavarsha, or defeated and driven it out from wherever it had secured a foothold. Chandragupta, Vikramaditya, and Skandagupta had headed such a centre, and saved the motherland by hurling back the barbarians as soon as they came.

The second need of the situation was a forward policy which would have taken the war into the heartland of Islam, instead of being fought over the length and breadth of Bharatavarsha. But the Hindus during this period were afflicted by a fortress psychology. They waited for the invader till he arrived at Panipat, or shut themselves into citadels which could be stormed or starved into surrender while the unprotected populace outside was slaughtered. Nor did they ever pursue and destroy the invader even when he was defeated and made of flee. If the Chaulukyas of Gujarat had pursued and destroyed Muhammad Ghuri and his hordes when he was defeated by them in his first expedition in 1178 AD, he would not have come back to Tarain in 1191 AD. Again, if the Chauhans had pursued and punished Ghuri after his defeat in the first battle of Tarain, there would have been no second battle of Tarain, and perhaps no more Muslim invasion of India, at least for some time to come. The effectivenenss of a forward policy was demostrated first by the Marathas under Shivaji, and later on by the Sikhs under Banda

Bahadur. But that was against an Islamic state already established in India. Meanwhile, Islam had succeeded in doing very severe damage to the self-respect and self-confidence of Hindu society, particularly to the psyche of its elite.

The consequences of this damage to the Hindu psyche came to the surface during the days of the Mughal empire. Hindu generals like Mansingh Kacchwaha, Jaswant Singh Rathore, and Mirza Raja Jaisingh, to name only the most notable, proved their great calibre when employed by an alien imperialism. Hindu administrators like Raja Todarmal streamlined the revenue system of an alien state. But they could not use their abundant talents for establishing their own leadership in the service of their own nation. The Marathas who finally occupied Delhi in 1771 AD provide an excellent example of this loss of *elan*. They could not muster the courage to proclaim their own sovereignty over their own motherland, and continued to function in the name of a phantom whom they had themselves freed from British captivity. They were frightened of their own greatness. The notion of an independent nationhood no more informed their vision.

The third need of the situation was a policy of reciprocity which nations have to follow when they are faced with gangsterism. Islam was suffering from the high fever of self-righteousness, and was badly in need of some strong medicine. If the Islamic invaders had been made to understand that what they intended to do to Somnath could also be done to the Ka'bah, they would have paused to think and shed some of their self-righteousness. But Hindus never tried to cure Islam of its iconoclastic zeal. On the contrary, they used every opportunity to convince Muslims that their mosques, mazars, and khanqahs were absolutely inviolable. No wonder Muslims came to the conclusion that while Somnath was built from bricks and mortar, and the *Śivaliṅga* made of mere stone, the Ka'bah was hewn out of some spiritual substance and the *sang-i-aswad* hallowed by the Almighty Allah. Muslims felt sure that while Hindu images had no power to protect themselves, their own idol in Mecca was capable of hurling into hell whole armies of infidels. Their sense of surety would have been shaken and done them immense good if it had been demonstrated by Hindu armies that the Ka'bah was also built from bricks and mortar, and that the *sang-i-aswad* also had no power to save itself, not to speak of sending even a mosquito to perdition.

Europe saved itself from the depredations of Islam because it had a centre in the Catholic Church which gave a call for action to Christian princes, and followed a forward policy in the Crusades. It did not allow Islam to retain any of its self-righteousness. Spain was ruled by Muslims for several centuries. But today there is no Muslim "minority" in Spain to poison its body politic, and no Muslim "places of worship" from which Muslim hooligans can hurl stones on Christian processions or in which they can assemble arsenals.

ISLAM IS STILL SELF-RIGHTEOUS

Islam in India is still suffering from the high fever of self-righteousness, though lately it has shifted its claim from the "only true religion" to the only "human brotherhood". Powered by petro-dollars, it is again dreaming of an empire in India. Hindus, on the other hand, have learnt no lesson from history as is evident from their slogan of *sarva-dharma-samabhāva* vis-a-vis Islam which is only a totalitarian and terrorist ideology of imperialism. And now the Hindu secularists are bent upon perverting the historical record in order to prove that Islam never intended any harm to Hindus or Hinduism! Will Hindu society have to pay the price again? It is highly doubtful if Hindu society will survive another determined assault from Islam, such is the mental, moral and spiritual health of this society.

A society which has no self-confidence, which suffers from self-pity, which indulges in breast-beating at the behest of every Hindu-baiter, and which stands in daily need of certificates of good conduct from its sworn enemies, has not the ghost of a chance in a world which is becoming deadlier with the passing of every day. Can such a society make any creative contribution to the greater good of mankind? Let every Hindu search his heart, and seek the answer.

CHAPTER X

THE STATUS OF HINDUS IN AN ISLAMIC STATE

Now I can take up the next NCERT guideline, namely, that historians cannot identify Muslims as rulers and Hindus as subjects, and that the state in medieval India under Muslim rule cannot be described as a theocracy without examining the role of religion in political conflicts.

I will take up the second half of this guideline first.

The modern apologists of Islam have been trying to rescue this "religion" from its macabre record as presented by the medieval Muslim historians. Firstly, they accuse the medieval historians of gross exaggeration. Secondly, they blame the Turks for barbarities committed in the name of Islam. The third pillar of this apologetics is to present as politically motivated the dismal deeds which the medieval historians regarded as religiously inspired.

AN EXAMPLE OF ISLAMIC APOLOGETICS

I have already analysed the first two approaches. An example will illustrate the third approach. M. Nazim writes in his well-known monograph, *The Life and Times of Sultan Mahmud of Ghazna:* "The critics who accuse the Sultan of wanton bloodshed and reckless spoliation of Hindu temples forget that these *so-called barbarities were committed in the course of legitimate warfare*, when such acts are sanctioned by the practices of all the great conquerors of the world. Spoils captured from the defeated enemy have always been considered lawful property of the victorious army. In India, however, wealth was accumulated not only in the coffers of the kings, as in other countries, but also in the vaults of the temples, which were consecrated in the service of various deities. The consequence was that, while elsewhere the capture of the defeated monarch's treasury usually gratified the conqueror's lust for mammon, in India temples were also ransacked to secure the piles of gold and precious stones in them. The religious considerations rarely carry weight with a conqueror, and the Sultan does not appear to have been influenced by them in his schemes of conquest." (emphasis added).

Nazim has a similar explanation for Hindu hostility to Islam. It is an essay in philosophy and sociology, as he understands them. He writes: "Some critics hold that a 'burning hatred for Islam was created in the Hindu mind because Islam was presented in the guise of plundering armies.' This view, however, is not convincing. The Hindus rejected Islam as their national religion because of the fundamental and irreconcilable differences between Islam and Hinduism. Islam with its definite articles of faith, could not appeal to the average Hindu to whom religion had never meant any specified set of doctrines. To regard an idol as a helpless piece of stone instead of a source of life and death, and to believe in one Omnipotent God instead of myriads of deities each one of which could be played against the other, was diametrically opposed to Hindu ways of thinking. *To this fundamental difference was added the hostility of the Brahmin, whose keen eye must have foreseen that the propagation of democratic principles of Islam would undoubtedly bring about a social revolution and break-down of the caste system on which depended his own exclusive privileges.* The Brahmins, therefore, as a class must have thrown the whole weight of their position against the spread of Islam. Besides this, hatred of change inherent in the Hindu mind would in any case have offered strong though passive resistance to the onward march of Islam." (emphasis added).

I am not commenting on the contradictions, prevarications, pretensions, and plain lies contained in these lines from a "learned historian" whose monograph was published by a prestigious British publisher. I am sure the readers will see for themselves the sheer scoundrelism of this apologetics. What I want to show in these quotations is the mind which the secularists in India have swallowed — hook, line, and sinker. It is this mind which our secularists have been cultivating over the years. And I am absolutely sure that the NCERT is out to patronise this mind.

POISON IN THE CORE OF ISLAM

What are the facts?

The seed is sown by the *Kalimah* — there is no god but

Allah and Muhammad is *the* prophet. This is not a religious precept which may be verified by spiritual experience, or referred to any system of logic. It is a purely political pronouncement which divides mankind into *mu'mins* and *kāfirs*, like the Communist division of people into "progressives" and "reactionaries", or the Nazi division of them into "superior" and "inferior" races.

Next, the Quran calls upon the *mu'mins* "to fight them till not a trace of unbelief is left", or "to fight those who do not profess the true faith till they pay *jizyah* with the hand in humility", or to "cut their throats wherever you find them", or you are no prophet until "you have made a great slaughter amongst them". This is called *jihād* (glorified as holy war) which is as fundamental a tenet of Islam as the *Kalimah, namāz, rozah, hajj,* and *zakāt*.

The Hadis and the four "pious" Khalifas elaborated the principles which are to be applied in *jihād* against those who do not accept Islam nor agree to pay *jizyah*. The infidel males capable of bearing arms are to be massacred; the infidel women and children are to be enslaved; the movable properties of the infidels are to be plundered; their lands are to be expropriated; their places of worship are to be destroyed; their priests and monks are to be killed and their scriptures burnt.

Those who agree to pay *jizyah* are to be treated as *zimmīs* who are allowed to live and work for the Islamic state under the following 20 disabilities: (1) they are not to build any new places of worship; (2) they are not to repair any old places of worship which have been destroyed by the Muslims; (3) they are not to prevent Muslim travellers from staying in their places of worship; (4) they are to entertain for three days any Muslim who wants to stay in their homes, and for a longer period if the Muslim falls ill; (5) they are not to harbour any hostility towards the Islamic state, or give any aid and comfort to hostile elements; (6) they are not to prevent any one of them from getting converted to Islam; (7) they have to show respect towards every Muslim; (8) they have to allow Muslims to participate in their private meetings; (9) they are not to dress like Muslims; (10) they are not to name themselves with Muslim names; (11) they are not to ride on horses with saddle and bridle; (12) they are not to possess arms; (13) they are not to wear signet rings or seals on their fingers; (14) they are not to sell or drink liquor openly; (15) they are to wear a distinctive dress which shows their inferior status, and which separates them from the Muslims; (16) they are not to propagate their customs and usages amongst the Muslims; (17) they are not to build their houses in the neighbourhood of Muslims; (18) they are not to bring their dead near the grave-yards of the Muslims; (19) they are not to observe their religious practices publicly, or mourn their dead loudly; and (20) they are not to buy Muslim slaves.

The "law" of Islam also prescribes death penalty for those who (1) question the exclusive claim of Islam as the *only true* religion, and of Muhammad as the *last* prophet; (2) try to revert to their ancestral faith after having been forced or lured to embrace Islam; and (3) marry Muslim women without first getting converted to Islam. Non-Muslims are also discriminated against in matters of testimony in law courts, taxation, and appointment to public offices. To sum up, the status of non-Muslims in an Islamic state is that of hewers of wood and drawers of water. They are subjected to every possible indignity and pressure in order to force them into the fold of Islam.

DEBATE OVER "ISLAM OR DEATH"

When an Islamic state was established over parts of northern India, the Ulama raised a great controversy. By now the interpreters of Islamic law had become divided into four schools — Hanafi, Hanbali, Maliki, and Shafii. The Hanafi school alone was in favour of extending the status of *zimmīs* to the Hindus. The other three schools were insistent that the only choice the Hindus had was between Islam and death. Ziyauddin Barani voiced his opinion against the Hanafi school when he wrote as follows in his *Fatwa-i-Jahāndāri:* "If Mahmud...had gone to India once more, he would have brought under his sword all the Brahmans of Hind who, in that vast land, are the cause of the continuance of the laws of infidelity and of the strength of idolators; he would have cut off the heads of two or three hundred thousand Hindu chiefs. He would not have returned his Hindu-slaughtering sword to its scabbard until the whole of Hind had accepted Islam. For Mahmud was a Shafiite, and according to Imam Shafii the decree for Hindus is Islam or death, that is to say, they should either be put to death or accept Islam. It is not lawful to accept *jiziya* from Hindus who have neither a prophet nor a revealed book."

Shykh Nuruddin Mubarak Ghaznavi was the most important disciple of Shykh Shihabuddin Suhrawardi, founder of the second most important sufi *silsilā* after the Chishtiyya, who died in Baghdad in 1235 AD. Ghaznavi had come and settled down in India where he passed away in 1234-35 AD. He served as *Shykh-ul-Islām* in the reign of Shamsuddin Iltutmish (AD 1210-1236), and propounded the doctrine of *Dīn Panāhī*. Barani quotes the first principle of this doctrine as follows in his *Tārīkh-i-Fīruzshāhī*: "The kings should protect the religion of Islam with sincere faith... And kings will not be able to perform the duty of protecting the Faith unless, for the sake of God and the Prophet's creed, they overthrow and uproot *kufr* and *kāfiri* (infidelity), *shirk* (setting partners to God) and the worship of idols. But if the total uprooting of idolatry is not possible owing to the firm roots of *kufr* and the large number of *kāfirs* and *mushriks* (infidels and idolaters), *the kings should at least strive to insult, disgrace, dishonour and defame the mushrik and idol-worshipping Hindus, who are the worst enemies of God and the Prophet.* The symptom of the kings being the protectors of religion is this:- *When they see a Hindu, their eyes grow red and they wish to bury him alive; they also desire to completely uproot the Brahmans,* who are the leaders of *kufr* and *shirk* and owning to whom *kufr* and *shirk* are spread and the commandments of *kufr* are enforced...Owing to the fear and terror of the kings of Islam, not a single enemy of God and the Prophet can drink water that is sweet or stretch his legs on his bed and go to sleep in peace." (emphasis added; read Allah for God).

Amir Khusru, the dearest disciple of Nizamuddin Awliya and supposed to be the pioneer of Secularism in India by India's secularist historians, echoed the same opinion when he wrote as follows in his *Khazāin-ul-Futūh* also known as the *Tārīkh-i-Alāī:* "The whole country by means of the sword of our holy warriors has become like a forest denuded of its thorns by fire. The land has been saturated by the waters of the sword, and the vapours of infidelism [Hinduism] have been dispersed. The strong men of Hind have been trodden under foot, and all are ready to pay tribute. Islam is triumphant, idolatry is subdued. Had not the law (of Hanifa) granted exemption from death by the payment of *jiziya*, the very name of Hind, root and branch, would have been extinguished."

The Muslim monarchs, however, knew better. They did not live in a fool's paradise like the mullahs and the sufis. The exponents of the "law" of Islam lived amidst leisure and luxury in towns protected by Islamic armies. They could very well afford to blow any amount of hot air about the "beauties" of their "religion". The Muslim monarchs, on the other hand, had to live mostly on the battlefields, and could feel in their guts the power equations of a situation in which they had to wage a constant war against stiff Hindu resistance and repeated reassertion of Hindu independence. They had discovered very soon that Hindus hated Islam as a system of black barbarism, and would fight rather than submit to this criminal creed. Moreover, they needed the Hindus for doing work which the mullahs, or the sufis, or the swordsmen of Islam were neither equipped for nor inclined to do — agriculture, commerce, industry, book keeping scavenging, and so on. No wonder the Muslim monarchs fell for the Hanafi school of Islamic "law" as soon as it was expounded to them, not because they liked this school but simply because they had no other choice. They recognized the Hindus as *zimmīs*, imposed *jizyah* and other disabilities on them, and reduced them, wherever they could, to the status of hewers of wood and drawers of water.

The mullahs and the sufis howled at this "sacrilege". Barani mourned: "Should the king consider the payment of a few *tankas* by way of *jiziya* as sufficient justification for their allowing all possible freedom to the infidels to observe and demonstrate all orders and detail of infidelity, to read the misleading literature of their faith, and to propagate their teachings, how could the true religion get the upper hand over other religions, and how could the emblems of Islam be held high? How will the true faith prevail if rulers allow the infidels to keep their temples, adorn their idols, and to make merry during their festivals with beating of drums and *dhols*, singing and dancing?"

THE STATE OF HINDU SOCIETY

But Barani and his likes were being unfair to the Muslim monarchs who were trying their best to serve Islam, *under the circumstances.* They were also painting far too rosy a picture of the condition of Hindu society in areas where the Islamic state had secured a stranglehold. Of course, the Hindus were singing and dancing in those parts of their motherland where their Rajas had retained or regained independence. But in areas controlled by the Muslim monarchs, Hindus had been turned into dumb driven cattle, always at the mercy of the meanest Muslim. Barani himself writes: "Sultan Alauddin (Khalji) demanded from learned men rules and regulations, so that the Hindu could be ground down and property and possession, which are the cause of disaffection and rebellion, could not remain in his house." One of these "learned men" was Qazi Mughisuddin. He advocated very stern measures and advised: "If the revenue collector spits into a Hindu's mouth, the Hindu should open his mouth to receive it without hesitation."

Alauddin Khalji raised the land revenue to one-half of the gross produce. He imposed a grazing tax on all milch cattle and a house-tax. Barani himself reports: "The people were brought to such a state of obedience that one revenue officer would string twelve *khuts, muqaddams* and *chaudharies* (all Hindus) together by the neck and enforce payment by blows." Hindus were so much impoverished that their wives had to work as servants in Muslim houses. Next came Alauddin's market regulations which our secularists and the All India Radio have been hailing as "the first experiment in socialism in India's history". The peasants, who were Hindus, were ordered to sell their grains to the merchants at arbitrarily fixed prices. The merchants, who were also

Hindus, were forced to sell this grain to the State, again at arbitrarily fixed prices which hardly left any margin of profit. There was so much grain stored in state godowns that Ibn Battutah who visited Delhi 18 years after Alauddin's death, ate rice which had been procured during Alauddin's reign. The Hindu merchants had to procure all sorts of merchandise from areas where there was no fixation of prices. But the prices at which they had to sell to the state were fixed without any reference to costs involved. And the merchants had to keep their wives and children as hostages at the capital to ensure that they brought regular supplies. This was expropriation, pure and simple, under conditions from which there was no escape except death.

Ghiyasuddin Tughlaq issued an ordinance which proclaimed that "there should be left only so much to the Hindus that neither on the one hand they should become intoxicated on account of their wealth, nor on the other should they become so destitute as to leave their lands and cultivation in despair". His son, Muhammad bin Tughlaq, enhanced the land revenue in a very steep manner. Barani reports: "The taxation in the Doab was increased ten and twenty times and the royal officials consequently created such *abwabs* or cesses and collected them with such rigour that the ryots were reduced to impotence, poverty and ruin... Thousands of people perished, and when they tried to escape, the Sultan led expeditions to various places and hunted them like wild beasts." Ibn Battutah who visited Delhi during Muhammad bin Tughlaq's reign, reports in his *Rehla* an Id celebration in the Sultan's palace: "Then enter the musicians, the first batch being the daughters of the infidel rajas captured in war that year. They sing and dance, and the Sultan gives them away to his amirs and *aizza*. Then come the other daughters of the infidels who sing and dance, and the Sultan gives them away to his relations, his brothers-in-law and the malik's sons." At a later date, "there arrived in Delhi some female infidel captives, ten of whom the vazir sent to me". Again, the Sultan sent to the emperor of China "one hundred male slaves and one hundred slave songstresses and dancers from among the Indian infidels". He also reports how the Muslim commandant of Alapur "would fall upon the infidels and would kill them or take them prisoner". The scoundrel was killed by the Hindus one day. His slaves fell upon Alapur, and "they put its male population to the sword and made the womenfolk prisoner and seized everything in it."

Firuz Shah Tughlaq organised an industry out of catching slaves. Shams-i-Siraj Afif writes in his *Tārīkh-i-Fīrūz Shāhī:* "The Sultan commanded his great fief-holders and officers to capture slaves whenever they were at war (that is, suppressing Hindu rebellions), and to pick out and send the best for the service of the court. The chiefs and officers naturally exerted themselves in procuring more and more slaves and a great number of them were thus collected. When they were found to be in excess, the Sultan sent them to important cities... It has been estimated that in the city and in the various fiefs, there were 1,80,000 slaves... The Sultan created a separate department with a number of officers for administering the affairs of these slaves."

Firuz Shah beat all previous records in his treatment of the Hindus. He himself writes in his *Futūhāt-i-Fīrūz Shāhī:* "The Hindus and idol worshippers had agreed to pay the money for toleration (*zar-i-zimmiya*), and had consented to the poll-tax (*jiziya*) in return for which they and their families enjoyed security. These people now erected new idol temples in the city and in the environs in opposition to the law of the Prophet which declares that such temples are not to be tolerated. Under divine guidance I destroyed these edifices, and killed those leaders of infidelity who seduced others into error, and the lower orders I subjected to stripes and chastisement, until this abuse was entirely abolished. The following is an instance. In the village of Maluh there is a tank which they call *kund.* Here they had built idol temples and on certain days the Hindus were accustomed to proceed thither on horseback, and wearing arms. Their women and children also went out in palankins and carts. There they assembled in thousands and performed idol-worship. The abuse had been so overlooked that the *bazar* people took out there all sorts of provisions and set up stalls and sold their goods... When intelligence of this came to my ears, my religious feelings prompted me at once to put a stop to this scandal and offence to the religion of Islam. On the day of the assembling I went there in person, and I ordered that the leaders of these people and the promoters of this abomination should be put to death... I destroyed their idol temples, and instead thereof raised mosques."

He records another instance in which Hindus who had built new temples were butchered before the gate of his palace, and their books, images, and vessels of worship were publicly burnt. According to him "this was a warning to all men that no *zimmi* could follow such wicked practices in a Musulman country". Afif reports yet another case in which a Brahmin of Delhi was accused of "publicly performing idol-worship in his house and perverting Mohammedan women leading them to become infidels". The Brahmin "was tied hand and foot and cast into a burning pile of faggots". The historian who witnessed this scene himself expresses his satisfaction by saying, "Behold the Sultan's strict adherence to law and rectitude, how he would not deviate in the least from its decrees."

Sikandar Lodi's "empire" was much smaller than that of Firuz Shah Tughlaq. But he enforced the "law" of Islam with no less zeal. A typical case of his reign is recorded by Abdulla in his *Tārīkhi-i-Dāūdī*: "It is related in the *Akbar Shahi* that there came a Brahman by name Bodhan who had asserted one day in the presence of Musulmans that Islam was true, as was also his own religion. This speech of his was aired abroad, and came to the ears of the *ulema*... Azam Humayun, the governor of that district, sent the Brahman into the king's presence at Sambal. Sultan Sikander ...summoned all the wise men of note from every quarter... After investigating the matter, the *ulema* determined that he should be imprisoned and converted to Islam, or suffer death, and since the Brahman refused to apostatize he was accordingly put to death by the decree of the *ulema*. The Sultan after rewarding the learned casuists, gave them permission to depart."

Hindu records of what the "law' of Islam meant to the Hindus are few and far between. But whenever they are available, they confirm the medieval Muslim historians. Gangadevi the wife of Kumar Kampana (died 1374 AD) of Vijayanagara writes as follows in her *Madhurāvijayam* regarding the state of things in the Madurai region when it was under Muslim rule: "The wicked *mlechchas* pollute the religion of the Hindus every day. They break the images of gods into pieces and throw away the articles of worship. They throw into fire *Srimad Bhagwat* and other holy scriptures, forcibly take away the conchshell and bell of the Brahmanas, and lick the sandal paints on their bodies. They urinate like dogs on the *tulsi* plant and deliberately pass faeces in the Hindu temples. They throw water from their mouths on the Hindus engaged in worship, and harass the Hindu saints as if they were so many lunatics let large."

Chaitanya-maṅgala, a biography of the great Vaishnava saint of medieval India, presents the plight of Hindus in Navadvipa on the eve of the saint's birth in 1484 AD. The author, Jayananda, writes: "The king seizes the Brahmanas, pollutes their caste and even takes their lives. If a conch-shell is heard to blow in any house, its owner is made to forfeit his wealth, caste and even life. The king plunders the houses of those who wear sacred threads on the shoulder and put scared marks on the forehead, and then binds them. He breaks the temples and uproots *tulsi* plants...The bathing in Ganga is prohibited and hundreds of scared *asvattha* and jack trees have been cut down."

Vijaya Gupta wrote a poem in praise of Husain Shah of Bengal (1493-1519 AD). The two qazi brothers, Hasan and Husain, are typical Islamic characters in this poem. They had issued orders that any one who had a *tulsi* leaf on his head was to be brought to them bound hand and foot. He was then beaten up. The peons employed by the qazis tore away the sacred threads of the Brahmans and spat saliva in their mouths. One day a mullah drew the attention of these qazis to some Hindu boys who were worshipping Goddess Manasa and singing hymns to her. The qazis went wild, and shouted: "What! the *harāmzādah* Hindus make so bold as to perform Hindu rituals in our village! The culprit boys should be seized and made outcastes by being forced to eat Muslim food." The mother of these qazis was a Hindu lady who had been forcibly married to their father. She tried to stop them. But they demolished the house of those Hindu boys, smashed the sacred pots, and threw away the *pūjā* materials. The boys had to run away to save their lives.

This was the state of things in those parts of India which were ruled by Muslim monarchs ever since Qutbuddin Aibak set up his first Islamic state in Delhi in 1206 AD. Punjab upto the Ravi and the whole of Sindh had passed under Muslim rule during the days of Mahmud Ghaznavi. Kashmir met the same fate early in the 14th century. If the state which treated the Hindus in such an abominable manner out of religious inspiration was not a theocracy, the NCERT "experts" would have to redefine the concept of theocracy. In common parlance so far, theocracy has meant the dominance of a single creed over the state apparatus, and discrimination against those who do not subscribe to that creed. Scoundrels like M. Nazim and Hindu secularists who preside over our education and "national integration", have tried to invent political explanations for measures which the Muslim monarchs adopted purely out of religious zeal. But in that case politics as well as religion miss their common parlance meanings, and become esoteric terms which scoundrels and secularists alone can decipher.

THE MYTH OF AKBAR

It is curious but true that the very historians who refuse to see the pre-Akbar period of Muslim rule as a nightmare for Hindus, hail Akbar as the harbinger of a dazzling dawn for the same Hindus. They point out as to how Akbar abolished the pilgrim tax and the *jizyah*, how he appointed Hindus to high positions, and how he extended to them this or that concession which they had not enjoyed earlier. One may very well ask these worthies that if these discriminatory taxes and disabilities did not exist earlier, how come you find Akbar freeing the Hindus from them? All that one is bound to get by way of an answer will be another bundle of casuistry.

There is no dearth of Hindu historians who heap Akbar with the choicest encomiums. Ashirbadi Lal Srivastava is a typical example. Pandit Jawaharlal Nehru goes much further and proclaims Akbar as the father of Indian nationalism. A Hindu who takes all these high-sounding stories with a pinch of salt, is rather rare nowadays.

On the other hand, most Muslim historians and theologians frown upon Akbar as a villain in the history of Islam in India. Ishtiaq Husain Qureshi who believes that Hindus were far more happy under Muslim rule than under that of their own princes, accuses Akbar of jeopardising Pax Moslemaica by tempering with the established tenets of Muslim polity. Maulana Abul Kalam Azad has written that if Ahmad Sirhindi had not come to the rescue, Akbar had almost finished Islam in India. It is only in post-Independence India that some Muslim historians have come forward to present Akbar as the pioneer of Secularism in this country. But we know what Secularism means in Muslim mouths, particularly if the Muslim happens to be a Marxist as well. For them, Akbar is no more than a Muslim hero for Hindu consumption.

One has, therefore, to go to the original sources in order to find the truth about Akbar. The story which these sources tell can be summed up as follows:

1. There was nothing Indian about Akbar except that he lived his life in India, fought his wars in India, built his empire in India, and dragged many Indian women into his harem. He knew nothing about India's spiritual traditions, or India's history, or India's culture except for what he heard from some native sycophants who visited his court for very mundane reasons. No Hindu saint or scholar worth his salt cared to meet or educate him about things Indian. It was only some Jain *munis* who came close to him. But then Jain *munis* have always been in search of royal patronage like the Christian missionaries. Moreover, Akbar used these *munis* for influencing some Rajput princes who would have otherwise remained recalcitrant.

2. Akbar was every inch an Islamic bandit from abroad who conquered a large part of India mainly on the strength of Muslim swordsmen imported from Central Asia and Persia. He took great pride in proclaiming that he was a de-

scendant of Taimur and Babur, and longed to recover the homelands of his forefathers in Transoxiana. He continued to decorate his name with the Islamic honorific *ghāzī* which he had acquired at the commencement of his reign by beheading the half-dead Himu. The wars he waged against the only resistant Hindu kingdoms — Mewar and Gondwana — had all the characteristics of classic *jihād*. Whenever he wanted to celebrate some happy event or seek blessing for some great undertaking — which was quite often — he went on a pilgrimage to the *dargah* of Muinuddin Chishti, the foremost symbol of Islam's ceaseless war on Hindus and Hinduism. He sent rich gifts to many centres of Muslim pilgrimage including Mecca and Medina, and carried on negotiations with the Portuguese so that voyages by Muslim pilgrims could be facilitated. In his letters to the Sharifs of Mecca and the Uzbek king of Bukhara, he protested that he was not only a good Muslim but also a champion of Islam, and that the orthodox Ulama who harboured doubts about him did not understand his game of consolidating a strong and durable Islamic empire in India.

3. The concessions which Akbar made to Hindus were not motivated by any benevolence towards Hindus or Hinduism on his part. He was out to win Hindu support in his fight with two inveterate foes of every Muslim empire-builder — the Muslim chieftains and the die-hard Ulama. Alauddin Khalji and Muhammad bin Tughlaq had faced the same foes earlier, but failed to overcome them because they could not break out of the closed circle of the foreign Muslim fraternity in India. Akbar succeeded in fixing both the foes because he tried a new method, and discovered very soon that it worked. He fixed the Muslim chieftains with the help of Rajput princes and their retinues. He fixed the Ulama partly by making them fall foul of each other in the Ibadat Khana, and partly by flirting with *jogis* and Jains *munis* and Christian missionaries in order to frighten them. They had nothing except royal patronage to fatten

upon. There is no evidence that Akbar's association with some spokesmen of rival religions was inspired by any sincere seeking on his part, or that the association improved his mind in any way. He remained a prisoner of Islamic thought-categories to the end of his days.

4. Nor did he have to pay a heavy price for Hindu support. Fortunately for him, he started functioning at a time when Hindu resistance to Islamic imperialism stood at a low ebb except in small pockets like Mewar and Gondwana. Hindu resistance had been led so far by the Rajput princes. But numerous wars fought by them with Muslim marauders for several centuries had exhausted their manpower as well as material resources. Akbar discovered it very soon that he could buy Rajput help in exchange for a few gestures which might have sounded ominous to orthodox Islam at that time but which proved only superficial in the long run. In fact, when one comes to think of it all, Hindus had to pay a very heavy price for those gestures from Akbar. He demanded Hindu princesses for his harem, which meant surrender of Hindu honour. He employed Hindu warriors not only against Muslim rebels but also against Hindu freedom fighters, which meant prostitution of Hindu heroism. For all practical purposes, he made the Hindus wield the sword of Islam not only in his own lifetime but right upto our own times. The pecuniary loss suffered by the Islamic state due to abolition of the pilgrim tax and the *jizyah* was compensated more than many times by the consolidation of an Islamic empire with a streamlined revenue system such as extracted from the Hindu masses, particularly the peasantry, the heavy cost of extending that empire by means of numerous wars, maintaining Mughal pomp and pageantry, and building monuments like the Taj. By the end of the Mughal empire, Hindu masses stood reduced to the subsistence level.

5. It was during the reign of Akbar that Muslim adventurers from many Islamic countries abroad started flocking towards India on an unprecedented scale, and made the Is-

lamic establishment in the country stronger than ever before. They occupied all the top positions in the army as well as the administration of the Mughal empire. Statistics may be marshalled in order to show that Hindu *share* in government posts went on increasing till the time of Aurangzeb. But there is no gainsaying the fact that Hindu *say* in the policies of the Mughal empire went on decreasing from the days of Akbar's immediate successor onwards. Even during the reign of Akbar, Muslim functionaries at the lower levels did not stop molesting Hindus in various ways normal to Islam. Many instances can be cited. Many a magnate in Akbar's court were in close contact with the orthodox Ulama and Sufis led by Shykh Ahmad Sirhindi who went about saying publicly that Hindu should either be made to embrace Islam or treated like dogs. They came out into the open as soon as Akbar was dead, and their progeny continued to progress towards renewed power and prestige from the reign of Jahangir onwards till they again rose to the top under Aurangzeb.

It is true that the main fault lay with the Hindus for not being able to see through Akbar's camouflage, and for helping him in consolidating an imperial power which Islam had never known in India in the pre-Akbar period of Muslim rule. But the fact remains that but for Akbar laying the firm foundations, there would have been no sadist scoundrel like Jahangir, no abominable criminal like Shah Jahan, and no Islamic monster like Aurangzeb for heaping endless torments and humiliations on Hindus. Let there be no doubt that far from being a dazzling dawn, the reign of Akbar was only the beginning of a darker night which continues till today in the form of Nehruvian Secularism.

Chapter XI
OF ASSIMILATION AND SYNTHESIS

Another major NCERT guideline regarding writing of medieval Indian history is that "neglect and omission of trends and processes of assimilation and synthesis, and growth of a composite culture" is "prejudicial to national integration".

The right hand does not know what the left hand has done. First, we are told not to treat the Islamic invaders as foreigners. Next, we are asked not to neglect trends and processes of assimilation and synthesis. One may very well ask: If the Islamic invaders were not foreigners, who was getting assimilated by whom? If the culture which these invaders brought with them was not alien, what was getting synthesised with what? And where is the need for inventing and sponsoring a composite culture, unless the Islamic culture is found to be working at cross purposes with the indigenous Hindu culture?

The Islamic invaders were not the first foreigners to come and settle down in India. In earlier times, the Iranians, the Greeks, the Parthians, the Scythians, the Kushanas, and the Hunas had also invaded India, and settled down here. There were some Mongolian incursions also in the north and the north-east. But by the time the Islamic invaders came to India, all these foreigners had been fully assimilated in the native population, and their cultures synthesised with the indigenous Indian culture. We have never had an Iranian, or a Parthian, or a Greek, or a Scythian, or a Kushana, or a Huna, or a Mongolian minority, or culture, or problem.

On the other hand, the Parsis came to India almost at the same time as the Muslims. They have remained a distinct minority with their own characteristic culture. It has never occurred to any historian, or sociologist, or politician to talk of the assimilation of Parsis in the native Hindu population, or of the synthesis of Parsi culture with Hindu culture. Till the other day, we had a Jewish minority which had kept its racial and cultural identity intact for almost two thousand years without creating any social, political, or cultural problem for the Hindus. The Syrian Christians in South India were another religious and cultural minoity which was carved out of the native population by early Christian missionaries, and which never threatened or felt threatened by the local people till the miliant missionaries who started coming with the dawn of Western imperialism, began instigating them for mischief.

The point that I want to emphasis is that it is not necessary for different racial groups to get assimilated, or for different cultures to get synthesised before they can live in peaceful co-existence. It is only when a culture is exclusive, intolerand, and aggressive that peaceful coexistence runs into deep waters.

MUSLIMS ARE A PROBLEM EVERYWHERE

It is not in India alone that the indigenous population has found it well-nigh impossible to co-exist peacefully with the Muslims. Greece had the same problem till it expelled its Muslim population. Yugoslavia and Cyprus in the West and the Philippines in the East, have an unsolved Muslim problem till today. Spain has no Muslim problem because it did not allow Muslims to remain within its borders after it defeated its Muslim invaders in a struggle spread over several centuries. Russia and China have 'solved' their Muslim problem for the time being in quite another way — by massive terror and ruthless suppression. One wonders for how long the experiment would survive.

On the other hand, no country where Islam has attained un-rivalled power has allowed non-Muslim minorities to survive. The Jews and the Christians were given the status of *zimmīs* by the Prophet himself. But what has happened to them in the lands of their birth? The Jews have been finally driven out from all Islamic countries after having suffered persecutions and humiliations in silence over the centuries. The Christian minority has met the same fate. Whatever Christian minorities have managed to survive, as in Egypt and Lebanon, they are having a very hard time at the hands of the latest wave of what is described as Islamic fundamentalism. There are no Zoroastrians in Iran any more. One wonders how long the Hindus of Bali and Malaysia will survive the renewed Islamic offensive powered by petro-dollars. The Hindus of Bangladesh, for establishing which the Hindus shed their own blood, are being harassed and hounded out.

The ruling class of secularists and socialists in India is trying to solve the Muslim problem by concocting a composite culture which, in their opinion, started taking shape in medieval India in the aftermath of Islamic invasions and in course of the Muslim rule. I wish them success. But I seriously doubt that the concoction will ever become a concrete reality.

WHERE IS THE COMPOSITE CULTURE?

The patron saint of India's secularism, Pandit Jawaharlal Nehru, saw the seeds of this composite culture sprouting in Muslim harems to which a large number of Hindu women had been dragged by force. The proposition is too preposterous to invite comment. Native women have always been a game for foreign invaders. The process would have had some meaning if the Hindu women had been allowed to retain their ancestral religion, or, better still, if Hindu men also had been permitted to marry Muslim women. Many Muslims in India today have one side of their ancestry in the helpless Hindu women of medieval India. But how many of them take pride in the Hindu part of their parentage? A one-way street should not be termed a two-lane highway.

Another bird of the same feather has come out with the 'bright" idea that Hindu employees of the Muslim state in medieval India and even some Hindu rulers and rich men had started donning Muslim dresses, adopting Muslim mores and manners, and patronising Persian language and literature. But even at its best, it was only cultural imposition or imitation. Here also the relevant point is: Did the Muslim invaders, except a microscopic minority, don any Hindu dress, or adopt any Hindu mores and manners, or patronise any indigenous language and literature? In any case, social usages like early marriage and *purdah* which Hindus learnt from the Muslims can hardly be called "culture". Something can be said in favour of *pān* which Muslims took from the Hindus, and *hennah* which Hindus took from the Muslims. But they are not very significant parts of Hindu or Muslim culture. The same is true of *halwā, sherbat, gulqand, achkan, chapkan, chapātī, kharbūzā,* and *tarbūz.*

Some other stalwarts of the same secular tribe point towards many social and cultural traits which were Hindu in their origin and which many Muslims in India, particularly its peasant and artisan communities, display at present. They forget that the vast majority of Muslims in India are Hindu converts who have retained many native customs even after they were forced or lured into the fold of Islam. For this failing of theirs, the native Muslims have always been despised by their *ashrāf* (Muslims of foreign descent) co-religionists, in spite of all the tall talk of Islamic brotherhood. The mullahs have been constantly mounting campaigns of *tablīgh* to cleanse the "native" Muslims of the remnants of *jāhiliyya.* India has known quite a few movements trying to finish the unfinished job — Islamizing the converts so completely that not a trace of their earlier Hindu culture remains in either their consciousness or outer way of life.

NOT IN ARCHITECTURE

Some champions of composite culture go into a trance over the synthesis of Hindu and Muslim architectural traditions. The Muslim rulers built many mosques, *mazārs, khānqahs,* palaces, and picnic spots. The materials used in these monuments had to be of Indian origin. The skills employed at the lower levels were also that of the native masons and labourers. These monuments, therefore, have quite a few features of the Hindu architectural styles. On the other hand, some Hindu rulers and rich men also built some monuments with domes and true arches — the two elements of architecture which Muslims had borrowed from the Byzantine empire and brought to India. But foreign rulers everywhere have always used native materials, native skills, and even native styles to build monuments which portray their power and wealth. And some native subjects have always tried to tread in the footsteps of their foreign masters.

Whatever synthesis and assimilation has gone into the making of these monuments has taken place at the purely physical level, and is entirely a result of outer circumstances. I thought that assimilation and synthesis meant some inner fusion, some psychological process also. Some Hindu temples or *samādhis* of Hindu saints built or even sponsored by some Muslim monarchs would have been significant signs of synthesis. But we search in vain for such signs. On the other hand, we find many mosques, *mazārs*, *khānqahs*, and palaces built over the sites and out of the debris of deliberately demolished Hindu temples, *samādhis*, *vihāras*, and palaces. And it is hard to find a mosque or a *mazār* built in the style of a Hindu temple or *samādhi*, which is quite significant.

NOR IN PAINTING, MUSIC, OR DANCE

Muslims in India hardly patronised any painting till the time of the Mughals. But the Mughal miniatures are purely Persian even when painted by Hindu artists, or patronised by Hindu princes. The Rajput and other Hindu schools of painting breathe an entirely different spirit, and draw their inspiration from an altogether different source. There is no synthesis, or assimilation, or even mutual influencing here.

It is only in the field of Hindustani music that we find Hindus and Muslims sharing the same tradition. But the fact that many Muslims specialise in this music does not make it Islamic. Islam has never had any music of its own. What is known as Hindustani music today has always been and remains Hindu music. Simply because some Hindu musicians converted to Islam in order to obtain patronage, does not mean that their music also underwent a similar conversion. *Qawwālī* music patronized by sufis is perhaps the only contribution of Islam. But it has remained confined to Muslim society, particularly Muslim *dargahs* and *mazārs*. Hindus sing their own *bhajans*, in their own diction and style, in their own places of worship.

The same is true in the field of dance and drama. The major schools and styles remained purely Hindu even when Muslim princes patronised them. *Mujrah* performed by prostitutes is perhaps the only Muslim contribution, patronised by both Hindu and Muslim profligates. For the rest, all folk dances and folk dramas all over India — the *swāng,* the *bhangrā,* the *jātrā,* the *nautankī,* the *tamāshā,* the South Indian stage — are entirely Hindu in dress as well demeanour. It is quite a different matter that Muslim masses enjoy them whole-heartedly even when the mullahs frown upon them. The presence of Muslim audiences at these performances proves nothing so far as composite culture is concerned. It means only that Muslim masses retain some Hindu tastes in spite of conversion to Islam.

NOR IN SCIENCE, OR LITERATURE

Muslims had always a lot to learn from the Hindus and very little to teach in the field of science. The only major science they brought with them was the Greek system of medicine. But Hindus were not quite unfamiliar with the system before the advent of Islam. Many Hindu *hakīms* specialised in this system of medicine, and many more Hindus benefitted from it over the years. It is a great science. But so is Ayurveda. What is significant in the present context is that we wait in vain to find a Muslim practitioner of this Hindu system of medicine, such has been the Muslim bias against most things Hindu. I wonder if a Muslim ever went to a *vaidya* unless absolutely unavoidable because a *hakīm* was not available.

The next secular historian compiles a list of Arabic and Persian translations of Sanskrit and Prakrit classics to conclude that Muslims and Hindus in medieval India travelled quite far towards one another. But none of these translations helped the Muslims to appreciate, far less to imbibe, any part of the Hindu spirit, or the Hindu cultural vision. Nor did these translations soften the Muslims towards the inheritors of such vast literary treasures, and regard them as anything better than despicable *kāfirs* and *kirāds.* Jayasi, Kutuban, Manjhan and some other sufis wrote their epics in Indian languages because they knew none of the languages patronised by Islam and, what is more important, because Islam had not yet corroded the cultural soul of these recent converts from the Hindu fold. I can cite several sufis who wrote in Indian languages but who invited Muslim monarchs to impose on the Hindus the disabilities decreed by the "laws" of

Islam. Muslims like Rasakhan were rare exception. Let us find a latter-day Muslim literatteur or sufi who has some kind words to say about such "renegades".

Hindu and Muslim literary traditions have been two separate streams which have hardly influenced one another. Indian languages have borrowed and assimilated many Arabic, Turkish, and Persian words. But these classic languages of Islam have remained, by and large, impervious to Hindu linguistic influences. They have kept every word of Indian origin at an arm's length. Urdu held some promise because its syntax as well as a large part of its diction had its roots in this land. But Muslims started claiming Urdu as the language of their culture, and the bridge that might have been built was destroyed. Over the years, this language has been heavily Arabicised and Persianised, and made more or less Greek for the Hindus at large.

MUCH LESS IN PHILOSOPHY AND RELIGION

Philosophy has never been a forte of Islam. Almost all its philosophical speculations have been borrowed from the Greeks, and borrowed very badly, because of the limitations imposed by the crudities of the Quran and the Hadis. But even this bit of borrowing has always invited severe indictment from the Ulama of Islam. Allama Iqbal was more than sure that Greek philosophy had corrupted and corroded the pristine purity of Islamic monotheism. And Muslim thinkers, by and large, have suffered from the same dread vis-a-vis Hindu schools of thought. Hindu monism was as much of an anathema to them as Hindu pantheism. On the other hand, Hindu philosophy throughout medieval India followed an independent course, free from any Islamic influence.

Our secular scholar feels on a firmer ground when he comes to the sufis and Hindu saints of the so-called *Nirguna* school. Here, he says, is a sure sign of synthesis, and that too at the highest level of human aspiration. But all those who have made a comparative study of the subject — Sufism and *Nirguna Bhakti* — are agreed that our secularist is making a serious mistake. It is significant that no *Nirguna* saint has mentioned the name of a single Indian sufi, while most of them have spoken warmly of earlier sufis like Rabia, Mansur Al-Hallaj, Junaid, Bayazid, Shams Tabrizi and Adam Sultan. This is because these earlier sufis were genuine mystics who lived before Islam was able too extinguished finally the spiritual traditions of Arab Paganism, Neo-Plantonism, Zoroastrianism, and Buddhism prevalent in the Middle East. The Ulama of Islam came down very heavily upon these earlier sufis as soon as the tone and temper of sufi poetry was noticed by the Ulema. Al-Gazzali worked out a compromise — the sufis could sing and dance or indulge in austerities provided they served Islam in its pursuit of world-conquest and world-conversion. It was not long before Sufism became an instrument of Islamic imperialism and terrorism. Even a sufi of the stature of Fariduddin Attar relates with great approval the following tale in his *Mantiq-ut-Tāir*: "It is said that when the Sultan (Mahmud Ghaznavi) captured Somnath and wanted to break the idol, the Brahmins offered to redeem it with its weight in gold. His officers pointed out to him the advantage of accepting the offer, but he replied: 'I am afraid that on the day of judgement when all the idolaters are brought into the presence of God, He would say, bring Adhar and Mahmud together; one was an idol-maker, the other an idol-seller.' The Sultan then ordered a fire to be lighted round it. The idol burst and 20 *manns* of precious stones poured out from its inside."

The sufi *silsilās* which travelled to India after the advent of Muinuddin Chishti were departments of the imperialist establishment of Islam. None of these sufis looked kindly at the Hindus, nor did the Hindus honour any of them with the exception of some simpletons who were taken in by the show of sufi piety, or some self-seekers who were out of curry favour with the Muslim courts with the help of sufis. Most sufis were like the later-day Christian missionaries whose animus against the Hindus is very well known. The *Nirguṇa* saints could not have been and were not impressed by them. In fact, some noted sufis are named in *Nirguṇa* poetry as shopkeepers and swindlers. On the other hand, the *Nirguṇa* saints constantly questioned the exclusive claims of Islam. They gave strength to Hindu society which the sufis were out of subvert and supplant.

To sum up this subject of synthesis, assimilation, and composite culture, I would better quote Dr. R.C. Majumdar, one of the best and certainly the most versatile historian which modern India has known. He writes: "There was no reapprochement in respect of popular or national traditions, and those social and religious ideas and beliefs and practices and institutions which touch the deeper chord of life, and give it a distinctive form, tone and vigour. In short, the reciprocal influences were too superficial in character to affect materially the fundamental differences between the two communities in respect of almost everything that is deep-seated in human nature and makes life worth living. So the two great communities, although they lived side by side, moved each in its own orbit and there was yet no sign that the twain shall ever meet." Again: "Nor did the Muslims ever moderate their zeal to destroy ruthlessly the Hindu temples and images of gods, and their attitude in this respect remained unchanged from the day when Muhammad bin Qasim set foot on the soil of India till the 18th century A.D. when they lost all political power."

The other day, an artist friend of mine told me an interesting story: "There was a painter who was fired by an irrepressible ambition to produce a female figure which would be the most beautiful when compared to all past and future performances in this field. He wandered all over the world visiting art galleries and studying poets and prose writers in many languages, in order to compile a collection of the most perfect female features — eyes, ears, nose, lips, chin, cheeks, bust, breasts, hips, and so on. Finally, he sat down to compose and paint the portrait. And it took him many more years to achieve the miracle..."

My friend fell silent at this point. I was agog with admiration, and asked him: "Where is this masterpiece? Can I see a facsimile of it in some book on art?" My friend smiled and said, "Sorry, I cannot help you. The artist destroyed his handiwork as soon as he had finished it, and then committed suicide." I was shocked and asked him — why? My friend replied: "Because the artist discovered that it was the most hideous composition which had ever come out of a painter's brush."

This is no more a matter of joke. The promoters of composite culture have been busy over the years in completing the job. They have gone a long way in dismembering Hindu culture and presenting its separate limbs as legacies of several socio-cultural streams — Austric, Dravidian, Aryan, Mongolian, Scythian, and so on. They will not rest till they have destroyed the unity of Hindu culture, and placed its components in such a juxtaposition as will look like a hideous patchwork. But that is not even half of the heart-rending story, They are bent upon forcing a marriage between Hindu and Muslim cultures. The end-product will surpass all possible horrors.

By all that I have written on the subject of composite culture, I do not intend to say that I am opposed to an understanding and reconciliation between the two communities. All I want to say is that no significant synthesis or assimilation took place in the past, and history should not be distorted and falsified to serve the political purposes of a Hindu-baiting herd. If there is any lesson which we can profitably learn from medieval Indian history, it is that no understanding between Hindus and Muslims is possible unless the very first premises of Islam are radically revised in keeping with reason, universality, and humanism.

A mere swelling of secular enthusiasm for Hindu-Muslim *Bhāi Bhāi* without analysing and eradicating the basic causes of conflict, has served only to harden the heart of Islam, and made it more self-righteous. None of our secularists has the stature or sincerity of Mahatma Gandhi in search of a settlement between Hindus and Muslims. In fact, our secularists have a vested interest in the Hindu-Muslim conflict which gives them their sense of superior heights as well as protects their self-seeking. But assuming that they are sincere like the Mahatma, they have no reason to harbour any illusion in a field where the Mahatma failed so staggeringly. The secularists should search their own minds and hearts, and study Hindu and Muslim cultures seriously rather than go on a wild goose chase in the pages of past history.

The mind of the secularists was exhumed by Dr. R.C. Majumdar in his Kamala Lectures delivered at the University of Calcutta in 1965. He said with great anguish: "In India today there is an Islamic culture as also an Indian culture. Only there is no Hindu culture. This word is now an untouchable (*apāṅkteya*) in civilised society. They very word Hindu is now on the way to oblivion. Because many people believe that this word symbolises a narrowness of mind and a diehard communalism."

CHAPTER XII

ISLAM VERSUS *INSĀNIYAT* (HUMANISM)

A few friends had expressed misgivings about my starting upon this series on the basis of a report in the *Indian Express.* They were apprehensive that in the process I may have been unfair to the NCERT.

A journalist friend has now kindly given me an authentic copy of *Guidelines And Tools For Evaluating School Text-books From the Standpoint of National Integration.* I have studied the mimeographed document and compared it carefully with the report in the *Indian Express.* I find that Mrs. Coomi Kapoor's reporting of the official position was fully faithful.

My heart sinks at the very idea of such a sinister scheme being sponsored by an educational agency set up by the government of a democratic country. It is an insidious attempt at thought-control and brainwashing. Having been a student of these processes in Communist countries, I have a strong suspicion that this document has also sprung from the same sort of mind. This mind has presided for long over the University Grants Commission and other educational institutions, and has been aided and abetted by the residues of Islamic imperialism masquerading as secularists.

India is not a clean slate on which any ideological language can be transcribed at will, even if the inscriber happens to be a leviathan which the state in India is increasingly tending to become. India happens to be a country with a hoary history. National memory and consciousness of cultural traditions instilled by that history can be ignored only if we are prepared to pay the price in terms of self-forgetfulness which will render the task of national integration well-nigh impossible.

PROPER BASIS OF NATIONAL INTEGRATION
A worthwhile climate for national integration can be created only on the basis of truth, justice, and a deeper perception of human culture. If we ignore these criteria and surrender to the unjust demands of intolerant ideologies, either because we are

impelled by temporary political expediency or because we are moved by a shallow and self-defeating Secularism, the result will inevitably be national disintegration, and, in the prevailing conditions of our encirclement by an aggressive Islamic Bloc, national enslavement.

Hindus were never very good political historians or biographers. Their historical interest was always centred on the life-stories of exceptionally outstanding heroes and saints, where also they enlarged the merely terrestrial in the image of the transcendent. One searches in vain the entire corpus of Itihasa-Purana for such historical data as the Greeks, the Romans the Chinese, and the Muslims have datelined about their kings and other luminaries. The three *Rājataranginis* written by Kalhana, Jonaraja, and Srivara are the only exceptions. What passes as Hindu political history before the advent of the Islamic invaders is mostly a patchwork pieced together by modern scholars out of epigraphic evidence, accounts of foreign travellers, and some indigenous literature. There is hardly anything in this history of India which needs correction except the perspective which has suffered substantial perversions, wittingly or unwittingly, during the days of the white man's supremacy.

It is only when we come to Islamic invaders of India that we have voluminous historical materials collected and compiled by hundreds of Muslim chroniclers. These materials have been carefully collated, compared, edited, annotated, and translated by a band of Western and Indian scholars. No one who is familiar with the results of this scholarship and wants to be fair can fail to vouchsafe that the scholars concerned have been, by and large, scrupulous and painstaking. It will be difficult to find significant instances of distortion and misrepresentation in this great endeavour, except when we come to the Stalinist "historians" like Mohammad Habib and Romila Thapar, to name only two from a fraternity which has multiplied fast under Nehruvian Secularism. It is not the fault of modern scholarship if the histories written by medieval Muslim historians are so damaging to the democratic, equalitarian, humanistic, and religious pretensions which Islam puts forth at present. The scholars have not invented any of the stories which sound so monstrous even after plenty of pruning away of what may be honestly held as poetic exaggeration.

Some other scholars have gone further and tried to find out if the monstrous deeds from which most Muslim monarchs, mullahs, and sufis derived such great satisfaction, are sanctioned by the basic tenets of Islam as expounded in the Quran, the Sunnah of the Prophet, and the sayings and doings of the first four pious caliphs. They have confirmed, more or less unanimously, that the enormities are enjoined by the scriptures of Islam in such an unequivocal language as leaves no scope for any misunderstanding whatsoever. The heroes of Islam can take legitimate pride that they have literally and very faithfully followed the teachings of Islam, and the legacy left by the Prophet and the pious caliphs.

A healthy and humanitarian system of education would have placed all these facts before our young men and women coming from the Muslim community, and put to them the following proposition: These are the words and deeds credited to Muslim kings, saints, and theologians by the historians of Islam in medieval India; these words and deeds compare very well with the words and deeds of Islamic kings, saints, and theologians in all other lands swept over by the armies of Islam; these words and deeds also conform quite closely to the tenets of Islam as expounded in the Quran and the Sunnah and the Shariat; we do not want you to evaluate these words and deeds and tenets in terms of any non-Islamic religion or culture; our only appeal to you is to evaluate them in terms of natural human reason, man's natural moral sense, and elementary principles of human brotherhood without resort to the casuistry marshalled by the mullahs and sufis, or the apologetics propped up by the Aligarh and Stalinist schools of historians; you have in you as much of the rational and the moral in human nature as the young men and women belonging to any other community; we wait for your verdict.

I am quite hopeful that approached in this manner most Muslim young men and women are likely to respond in a positive manner. At least a good beginning would have been made in opening up the minds and hearts of these young people to normal human values, and leading them out of the prison-house of Islam in which most Muslims have lived over the past so many centuries. Muslims in India as elsewhere have been living in a Dark Age ever since they were forced or lured into the fold of Islam, the same way as the Christians in the West had lived during the medieval period presided over by the Catholic Church. Christians in the West experienced an Age of Reason and Renaissance when they processed Christian doctrines and history in terms of rationalism and humanism, and reawakened to some extent to their ancient pagan heritage. There is no reason why the Muslims in India and elsewhere should not experience the same reawakening, once they recover the ancient cultural traditions of their respective countries, and start standing by rationalism and humanism.

IS ISLAM A RELIGION?

Some people are prone to confuse Islam with its victims, that is, the Muslims, and condemn the latter at the same time as they come to know the crudities of the former. This is a very serious confusion, which should be avoided by all those who believe in building up a broad-based human brotherhood as opposed to narrow, sectarian, self-centred, and chauvinistic nationalism or communalism. Let there be no doubt that an average Muslim is as good or bad a human being as an average Hindu or, for that matter, any average person belonging to any race, religion, or culture. What concerns us here is the worth of Islam as an ideology, and not the worth of Muslims as human beings.

This is not the occasion to discuss the deeper question whether Muhammad was a prophet, or whether what he claimed to be the Quran is a revelation from some divine source. I am also postponing for the time being, and leaving for better minds than my own, the discussion whether Islam is a religion or a political ideology of imperialism. Here I will only ponder over some of the persistent pretensions of Islam — pretensions which have so far remained unquestioned in this country or elsewhere.

The first pretension of Islam to which many learned or pious

people fall an easy prey is Monotheism as contrasted with Polytheism, that is, the pitting of 'True One God' against 'false many
gods'. The mere sound of the word 'monotheism' spreads such
a hypnotic spell over certain minds that they suspend their
thought operations, and refuse to look into the meaning and implications of this concept which is shared in common by the
three prophetic creeds — Judaism, Christianity, and Islam.

Ram Swarup has studied the scriptures of Christianity and
Islam, and meditated over Monotheism and Polytheism for a
number of years. I will reproduce below what he has to say on
this subject in his book, *The Word As Revelation: Names of
Gods:*

" The fact is that the problem of One or Many Gods is born
of a theological mind, not of a mystic consciousness. In the
Atharvaveda (2.1.1), the sage Vena says that he 'sees That in that
secret station of the heart in which the manifoldness of the world
becomes one form', or as in the *Yajurveda* (32.8) where the
'world is rested in one truth'. But in another station of man
where not his soul but his mind rules, there is opposition between the One and Many, between God and Matter, between
God and Gods. On the other hand, when the soul awakens, Gods
are born in its depths which proclaim and glorify one another.

"The Hindus do not call their Gods either 'One' or 'Many'.
According to them what they worship is One Reality, *ekam sat,*
which is differently named. This Reality is everywhere, in everything, in every being. It is One and Many at the same time and
it also transcends them both. Everything is an expression, a play,
an image, an echo of this Reality.

"Spiritual life is one but it is vast and rich in expression. The
human mind conceives it differently. If the human mind was
uniform without different depths, heights and levels of subtlety;
or if all men had the same mind, the same psyche, the same
imagination, the same needs, in short, if all men were the same,
then perhaps One God would do. But a man's mind is not a fixed
quantity and men and their powers and needs are different. So
only some form of polytheism alone can do justice to this variety
and richness.

"Besides this variety of human needs and human minds, the spiritual reality itself is so vast, immense and inscrutable that man's reason fails and his imagination and fancy stagger in its presence. Therefore, this reality cannot be indicated by one name or formula or description. It has to be expressed in glimpses from many angles. No single idea or system of ideas could convey it adequately. This too points to the need for some form of polytheism.

"A purely monotheistic God unrelieved by polytheistic elements tends to become lifeless and abstract. A purely monotheistic unity fails to represent the living unity of the spirit and expresses merely the intellect's love of the uniform and the general.

"In the cultural history of the world, the replacement of Many Gods by One God was accompanied by a good deal of conflict, vandalism, bigotry, persecution and crusading. They were very much like the 'wars of liberation' of today, hot and cold, openly aggressive or cunningly subversive. Success in such wars played no mean role in making a local deity, say Allah of certain Arab tribes, win a wider status and assume a larger role."

GOD AND THE NEIGHBOUR

Ram Swarup has further simplified the proposition and placed it in a social context in another work which is yet to be published. He says:

"In the spiritual realm there are two categories: God and your neighbour. And correspondingly there are two ways of looking at them: you could look at God through your neighbour or at the neighbour through your God. In the first approach, you will think that if your neighbour has the same needs and constitution and impulses as you have, then his God, in whatever way he is worshipped and by whatever name he is called, must mean the same to him as your God means to you. In short, if your neighbour is as good as you are, his God also must be as good as yours.

"But if you look at your neighbour through your God, then it leads to an entirely different outlook. Then you say that if your

God is good enough for you, it should be good enough for your neighbour too. And if your neighbour is not worshipping the same God in the same way, he must be worshipping Devil and qualifies for conversion or liquidation.

"The first approach promotes tolerance, though it gives a plurality of Gods and varieties of modes in worship. The other approach gives one God and one mode of worship, but breeds intolerance. The one idea tries to generalise itself through conquest and calls itself the truly one, the truly universal."

MONOTHEISM IS DISGUISED MATERIALISM

If the theologians of Christianity and Islam can be considered authoritative exponents of Monotheism, it means that God or the Supreme Power or whatever the name we give to the Ultimate Reality, remains outside the Cosmos, that is, becomes extra-cosmic after the act of Creation. These theologians praise God as Omnipotent and Omniscient, but frown at any association of Omnipresence with Him. The very thought that God could be present in the human heart (*antarayāmin*), in the Universe (*sarvanivāsin*), in Nature, in animals, in plants, and even in matter is denounced by them as Pantheism which, according to them, is as great, if not greater, a blasphemy as atheism itself. Islam denounces Polytheism as *shirk*, that is associating creatures with the Creator, which, according to it, is the same as thing as seeing God's presence in his creation.

Looked at in this manner, an inescapable implication of Monotheism is that the Cosmos is completely denuded of any inherent Divinity, and made very, very material. There is no divinity inherent in human beings, or animals, or in material things. Monotheism thus becomes a disguised form of Materialism. What is worse, it leads to the lowest type of idolatry because it places God at the mercy of an historical person, hailed as the Prophet or the Son on whom the extra-cosmic deity must depend for communicating with his creatures. Songs and sermons in praise of a Jesus or a Muhammad soon surpass the hymns addressed to God Almighty.

ALLAH IS AN EGO-GOD

The Allah of Islam is not even a monotheistic God of the initial Biblical conception. On the contrary, it is what Ram Swarup calls an Ego-God:

"The Upanishads say that God chooses whom he will. This is true in a deeper sense. It means that He is beyond our choices and preferences, our likes and dislikes, and our conceptions of Him, or definitions of right and wrong, false and true.

"But there is a sense in which we choose our own Gods. God made man in His own image. But man also makes God in his own image. Our God is what we are. If our heart is pure, our God is also pure, but if our hearts are impure, our Gods too are impure.

"Most men want a God who humours them and gratifies them, who vindicates and justifies their way of life, who sanctifies them in their own eyes and in those of their friends...They want their kingdom to extend, they want war-booty, particularly in the form of gold and young girls; they want their enemies to be slain and humbled.

"Ego-Gods come fully into their own when our desires take on moral and theological disguises: when the Ego uses a higher principle for a lower satisfaction, the truth itself is perverted and Ego-Gods are born. We worship the Ego-Gods when we worship the lower in the higher."

This is the true import of the *Kalima* — there is no god but Allah and Muhammad is *the* Prophet. It seems that the prophet of Islam had no use for a God who could have his own independent will, who could have and express his own opinions of men and matters, and who could exercise his own judgement about right and wrong. On the contrary, the Prophet needed a proxy disguised as god who would echo precisely, though in a pompous language, the personal proclivities of the Prophet in every situation, domestic as well as public, which the Prophet had to face. This conclusion is confirmed by a reading of the Quran in a chronological order, side by side with the orthodox biographies of the Prophet. The close correspondence between what the Prophet was planning or pining for in his normal moments, and what was revealed to him in a state of *wahy* that followed soon after, is quite striking. The chronological confusion in the compilation of the Quran has helped a good deal to hide this correspondence.

So much for the first pretension of Islam.

BROTHERHOOD OF BANDITS

The second pretension of Islam is that it stands for human brotherhood and social equality as contrasted with the caste divisions and class hierarchies rampant in other societies, particularly the Hindu society. Many people with socialist preferences or pretensions are duped by what they describe as the "social progressivism" of Islam. We have in this country a whole battalion of Hindu-baiters who have no use for Allah or for Muhammad but who strongly recommend Islam on the rebound because they have come to believe that Islam stands for better social values. And there is no dearth of Hindus, who, while they love their own religion and culture, admit at the same time that Hindu society has a lot to learn from Islam in matters of brotherhood and equality.

Islam had never put forward these claims before the rise of democracy and socialism in modern times. The old theologians of Islam were meticulous in placing various people in their proper places. The *mu'mins* (believers) constituted the master class (*millat*) entrusted with the mission of imposing the faith and law of the Prophet on all mankind. The *kāfirs* were the scum of the earth who were to be consigned to eternal hell-fire whenever they could not be killed or converted outright. The *zimmīs* were people who accepted the supremacy of the Islamic state and agreed to live as non-citizens under severe disabilities. The slaves were mere merchandise who could be bought and sold in the bazar, and killed without any compunction if they tried to escape into freedom. And the women (*zan*) were men's personal property comparable to gold and silver (*zar*) and land (*zamin*), to be kept veiled and hidden in the harem if they happened to be legal wives, or to be presented as gifts if they happened to be newly captured beauties, or to be circulated among friends if they happened to be concubines. Within the *millat* itself, the Quraish had primacy over the plain Arabs at the start of Islamic imperialism. The civil list devised by Caliph Umar for monetary grants given to Arab families out of the booty obtained in wars, reflects this class hierarchy in Arab society. As the Arab empire expanded east and west, the non-Arabs everywhere were treated as inferior people, in law as well as in practice, even when the latter became *mu'mins*. Later on, the Turks took over the Arab legacy of being a master race. Islam has never known any brotherhood or equality even within its *millat*.

But the theologians of Islam look the other way when Islam gets sold in a new garb, and that too by people who do not profess Islam. They are also prepared to participate in the crudest casuistry in interpreting the Quran in line with the latest demagogies of social philosophy. The "only true faith" has to be served even if it means a fraud on the "hallowed scripture".

The Quran is quite frank and straight-forward on the subject of human brotherhood and social equality. It says: He who seeks a faith other than Islam will never be accepted (3.85). You fight them till not a trace of unbelief is left (8.39). When you meet the *kāfirs*, cut their throats until you have made a great slaughter amongst them, and when you have defeated them, take them prisoners so that you may earn ransom. Fight them till they surrender (47.4). War is prescribed for you, and you dislike. But it is possible that you dislike what is good for you (2.216). And so on, it all reads like a manual of war on mankind rather than a charter of human brotherhood. It neatly divides humanity into *mu'mins* and *kāfirs*, and leaves not the slightest scope for any mutual understanding or normal morality between the two.

So much for the second pretension of Islam.

ISLAM BRUTALISED ARAB SOCIETY

The third pretension of Islam is that it rescued Arabia from an era of darkness (*jāhiliyya*), and put her squarely on the path of cultural progress. The proposition needs a very close examination. No records of pre-Islamic culture have survived except a bit of poetry, which by itself is a telling evidence of the havoc wrought by Islam on a society whose only fault was that it did not take seriously the prophethood of Muhammad. Even so, something of the pre-Islamic Arab society and culture shines through the lies told about them by the biographers of Muhammad. It was a tribal society no doubt. But the tribes had a long tradition of large-hearted religious liberalism which made the worshippers of many Gods and Goddesses live peacefully side by side. The Jews and the Christians also enjoyed full religious freedom in this environment of tolerance and understanding. It was this liberalism and tolerance which permitted the prophet of Islam to preach and practise all that he did. If pre-Islamic Arab society had been what Islam made of it after Muhammad's mailed fist had triumphed, there would have been no prophet and no Islam.

The pre-Islamic Arabs were honest in their dealings with other people, and chivalrous towards their enemies. They practised a code of honour in all give and take. The women in pre-Islamic Arabia had a very high status. They presided over business and commerce. They took part in public debates and poetic contests. They rode freely by themselves for visiting friends and lovers. They accompanied and stood by their men on the field of battle. They never wore the veil which Islam forced on them.

It was this simple, straight-forward, and essentially human society which Islam divided by mutual hatred sown by a monopolist of "divine revelations". Brother was turned against brother, sons and daughters against parents, wives against husbands, and neighbour against neighbour. A ruthless gang of wholetime hoodlums was let loose on this society by a preacher of "perfect virtue". This gang led many surprise expeditions against unsuspecting tribal settlements without any provocation whatsoever, looted caravans which were not expecting to be waylaid, massacred many innocent men and women and children in the most cruel manner, enslaved many more who had always been free citizens, forced many helpless women into slavery and concubinage, and deprived whole communities of their inherited as well as hard-earned properties, movable and immovable. The victims were at first baffled by this unprecedented and uncivilised conduct on the part of those whom they regarded as their own kith and kin. They fought back half-heartedly when their patience was exhausted. And they surrendered to superior military strategy and armed force which they had neither the time nor the resourcefulness to match.

The Arab people were brutalised after Islam destroyed their ancient and humane culture, and forced them to fulfil its fiendish behests. The Arab people now became a brotherhood of bandits who fell like hungry wolves on the neighbouring lands, who massacred other people *en masse* in the name of Monotheism, who desecrated and demolished other people's places of worship in the name of Allah, who looted and pillaged whole countries and pupulated them with bastard progenies begotten on helpless native women without number, and who carried away whole masses of men and women and children and sold them into slavery. This "civilising" mission of Islam was taken over by the Turks at a later stage, particularly in India.

It is high time that we see through the pretensions of a pernicious political ideology masquerading as religion, and expose the truth which is being suppressed by the hawkers of Nehruvian Secularism. It is high time that the Muslims everywhere are made to know that Islam has been and remains as far from *Insāniyat* as the North Pole from the South Pole. The Dark Night which dwells over many lands invaded by Islam and which is trying to spread farther afield with the help of petro-dollars, has to be rolled back till every Muslim receives his normal share of daylight. A beginning of this mission can be made in India, the land of Sanātana Dharma.

But before we set out to accomplish that mission, we have to use discretion in defining what is *dharma*. We should not sloganise the truths of Sanātana Dharma as is evident when we practise *sarva-dharma-sama-bhāva* vis-a-vis Islam and Christianity.

APPENDIX

(These articles appeared in the weekly *Organiser* and invited some comments from the readers, particularly Dr. K.K. Mittal with whom I developed almost a debate spread over several issues of the weekly. I discovered that Dr. Mittal had equated Islam with Urdu poetry with which he happened to be in love. The following questions from Sindhu, the pseudonym used by the editor, Shri K.R. Malkani, and the answers I gave are relevant to this book.)

ANY SILVER LINING?
(Sindhu, New Delhi)

I have been following the Sitaram Goel series — and the Goel-Mittal Debate — with much interest.

I agree with the intent of both, Shri Goel and Shri Mittal.

Shri Sitaram is only recapitulating recorded history. But the account makes such sad reading that Dr. Mittal tries to see some silver linings. Maybe he is only looking in a dark room for a black cat, that is not there. But the effort is laudable.

Shri Goel is speaking the truth and nothing but the truth. But is it the "whole truth"? Is it possible that Muslim rule was not all jet-black — but also part-gray?

According to Max Weber, more 'tribals' joined the Hindu mainstream as a result of the Muslim shock, than the number of Hindus who converted to Islam.

As a friend once put it, it was in reaction to Muslims we became "Hindus"; and it was in reaction to the British that we became "Indians".

While Hindu rulers through much of history contented themselves with local hegemony, few of them had any idea of the political unity of India. On the other hand, even regional Muslim chieftains were always trying to expand and, if possible, to capture the centre. Could this be interpreted as a contribution to the political unity of India?

A centralised State under the Sultans created a huge Common Market. Did this encourage trade and industry?

When Europeans arrived in India, they found Delhi and Agra much bigger and richer than London and Paris. Would this have been the case if Muslim rule had been an unmitigated evil?

Even during Muslim rule, we produced great poets like Tulsi, Mira, Sur, Kabir — apart from innumerable Sufi saint-poets. Why are these poets silent about Muslim misrule? Is it because even the misrule was governed by a certain rule of law?

I do not know. But perhaps Shri Goel, Dr. Mittal and other friends could enlighten us all on these and other related points.

MUSLIM RULE HAD NO SILVER LINING
(Sita Ram Goel)

Sindhu has raised certain questions in the *Organiser* dated April 11-17, which I should like to answer. I may, however, state my final conclusion first — Muslim rule in India was an unmitigated evil.

1. I have never read Max Weber and do not know how he has arrived at the conclusion that "more tribals joined the Hindu mainstream as a result of the Muslim shock than the number of Hindus who were converted to Islam". Perhaps he had in mind the people of Assam whom Bakhtyar Khalji and a few other Muslim invaders tried to subjugate, or the hill people all over our northern borders whom Muhammad Tughlaq tried to conquer but failed, or the Gonds who fought Akbar under Maharani Durgavati, or the Bhils who fought for freedom under Maharana Pratap, or the Mavlas who joined Shivaji at a later date. But the very fact that these so-called "tribals" fought spontaneously against the Muslim marauders rather than walk over to the winning side goes to prove that they shared a common culture with the rest of the natives. Of course, the term "Hindu" can be defined in a narrow manner to mean people within the fold of *Varṇāśrama* in which sense the so-called tribals were not the so-called Hindus. But that is only proving what one has already assumed. A Hindu should not walk into that trap.

2. It is true that the natives of Bharatavarsha became known as Hindus to themselves only after the Islamic invasion, as they were known earlier only to the foreigners. But that was not a

happy outcome which we could welcome. We were a great culture before the Muslims came to this country — the culture sustained by Sanātana Dharma. The Muslim invasion converted us into a mere community which was now called upon to defend its very existence. We have to hug the term Hindu because Bharatavarsha now is also inhabited by communities which do not share the culture of Sanātana Dharma. We have to have a distinct identity of our own, however defective the name we choose or are forced by circumstances to choose, for ourselves. Moreover, the term Hindu has now become hallowed by association with countless heroes and martyrs who lived and died for Hindu Dharma and the Hindu homeland. Even so, it would be the beginning of a new dawn if we can win our alienated brethren back to their ancestral faith and become once again a single family sustained by Sanātana Dharma. The term Hindu will then become superfluous, and can be dropped.

3. Hindu rulers on the eve of Muslim invasion had not totally forgotten the idea of the political unity of India. The ancient tradition enshrined in the Mahabharata and the Puranas and honoured by Indian emperors as late as Samudragupta, namely, that the whole of Bharatavarsha was a *cakravartī-kshetra*, was still smouldering when many princes joined the Hindu Shahiyas in their fight against Subuktigin. But the tradition had become greatly weakened, though it did not die till 1947 when we accepted Partition and conceded to the aggressor the fruits of his aggression. Of course, the ancient idea of political unity was not the same as that brought in by Islam which has always stood for a monolithic and militarised state serving a system of an incurable fanaticism. Our concept of *sāmrajya* was derived from Sanātana Dharma and fostered a true federation of many *janapadas* enjoying *swarājya*, local autonomy, on the basis of *swadharma*, local tradition and culture. Islam made no contribution to the unity of Bharatavarsha; on the contrary, it seriously damaged the deeper fabric of our national unity and, in the final outcome, dismembered the nation into fragments like Afghanistan, Pakistan, Hindustan, Bangladesh, and Nepal.

4. The eulogisation of a common market is a capitalist-im-

perialist innovation. It only means that the common people in the interior who produce the wealth, are not permitted to enjoy it. The fruits of their labour, enterprise, and skill are taken away from them by tampering with the terms of trade, and made available to a parasitic population in metropolitan centres; or, worse still, the common people in the interior are forced or lured to produce not what they need for themselves but what a parasitic urban population requires for a life of pofligacy and waste. The infrastructure created by the ancient culture of this country was informed by the spirit of *swadeshi* — local materials, local techniques, and local labour are mobilised for the satisfaction of local needs, and only the surplus is sent out in exchange for useful goods from outside. The Muslim rule damaged this infrastructure to a certain extent under pressure from its parasitic court and aristocracy. But, by and large, it survived the Muslim rule till it was undermined to a great extent by inroads from British capitalism-imperialism. We are now dealing to it the final death blows by our five-year plans. Let us be fair to the Muslim rule in India. It did not create any significant centralised market, nor, consequently, did it damage very significantly the infrastructure which had proved an infallible source of strength throughout our long history.

5. The Europeans might have found Delhi and Agra bigger than London and Paris at that time. But what was Europe as compared to India till the end of the 18th century? It was a poor continent sending out large armies of its anti-social elements in search of loot under the banner of Christianity. Agra and Delhi should be compared with Pataliputra, Varanasi, Ujjain, Kanauj, Kanchipuram, Madura and Tanjore which flourished before the advent of Islam or even with contemporary Vijayanagara, to find out what a sorry figure the former make. These renowned seats of Muslim rule were small towns in comparison to the leading cities in ancient India. Moreover, all Muslim cities were networks of narrow slums which would have outraged the classical tastes of our ancient town planners. The layout of Mohenjo-daro is the oldest and that of Jaipur the latest specimen of what wide spaces entered the imagination of an urban culture which derived

its inspiration from an infinitude of the inner Spirit. The Muslim cities were mostly ghettos — the material manifestation of a spiritual ghetto which is Islam.

6. Sufis during the Muslim rule might have been poets. I cannot judge because I am no connoisseur of Persian poetry. But I seriously doubt if they were saints, except a few on whom Islam continues to frown even today. Nor were the sufis specific to India. Islam produced whole armies of them in all lands it invaded during its heyday. In any case, I cannot take pride in Indian sufis who were a part of the imperialist establishment of Islam. On the other hand, Muslim rule had nothing to do with the rise of Hindu saints like Kabir, Nanak, Tulsi, Sur and Mira. They arose in spite of Islam, and flourished only because Islam could not reach out to kill them. Shall we attribute the rise of Solzhenytsin to the rule of Stalin? Human spirit is unconquerable in the long run. Kabir and Nanak have referred to the inequities of Islam in very clear terms. Tulsi, Mira and Sur did not refer to Islam because it was beneath their contempt. At the same time, let us not forget that Mira flourished in Mewar which was never under Muslim rule, and Tulsi and Sur flourished under Akbar who had largely dismantled the edifice of the Islamic state in India and struck up a deal with the Rajputs. The misrule of Islam was of course governed by a rule of law — the "law" of Islam. But the "law" of Islam never became universal in India. How many Jewish, Christian, Zoroastrian and Buddhist mystics and saints flourished in lands where the "law" of Islam attained a universal sway?

I wonder if I have answered the 6 questions raised by Sindhu to his entire satisfaction. But this is the best I know.

Index